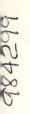
984299

GARNETT LIBRARY
SMSU-WEST PLAINS
Murrell Library
Missouri Valley College
Marshall, Missouri 65340

WITHDRAWN
from MSU-WP Garnett Library

27.-

RC 480.5 .K625 1995
Knights, Ben, 1947-
The listening reader

984299

The

Fiction and Poetry

D0141351

of related interest

Shakespeare as Prompter
The Amending Imagination and the
Therapeutic Process
Murray Cox and Alice Theilgaard
ISBN 1 85302 159 8

Structuring the Therapeutic Process
Compromise with Chaos: The Therapist's
Response to the Individual and the Group
Murray Cox
ISBN 1 85302 028 1

The Cradle of Violence
Essay on Psychiatry, Psychoanalysis
and Literature
Stephen Wilson
ISBN 1 85302 306 X

Imagery and Symbolism in Counselling
William Stewart
Volume 1. ISBN 1 85302 350 7

An A–Z of Imagery and Symbolism in Counselling
William Stewart
Volume 2. ISBN 1 85302 351 5

Murrell Library
Missouri Valley College
Marshall, Missouri 65340

The Listening Reader

Fiction and Poetry for Counsellors and Psychotherapists

Ben Knights

Jessica Kingsley Publishers
London and Bristol, Pennsylvania

Acknowledgements

Copyright material is reproduced by permission as follows:

Emily Dickinsons's poem 'One need not be a chamber' is reprinted by permission of the publishers and the Trustees of Amherst College from *The Poems of Emily Dickinson*, Thomas H. Johnson, ed. Cambridge, MA: The Belknap Press of Harvard University Press, copyright © 1951, 1955, 1979, 1983 by the President and Fellows of Harvard College.

U.A. Fanthorpe's poem 'After Visiting Hours' by kind permission of the author.

Nadine Gordimer's story 'The Train from Rhodesia' is reprinted from *The Selected Stories of Nadine Gordimer* by kind permission of the author and Jonathan Cape Publishers, UK and Viking Press, New York.

Tony Harrison's poem 'Fire-Eater' is reprinted by kind permission of the author.

Denise Levertov's poem 'To Speak' is reprinted from *Selected Poems* published by New Directions Publishing Corporation (UK rights) and from Denise Levertov: *Poems 1960–1967* copyright © 1960 by Denise Levertov (US and Canadian rights) by permission of the author and New Directions Publishing Corporation.

Stevie Smith's poem 'Anger's Freeing Power' is reprinted by kind permission of James MacGibbon.

William Carlos Williams' poem 'The Mind Hesitant' is reprinted from *Collected Poems* by kind permission of Carcanet Press Ltd (UK rights), and from William Carlos Williams: *Collected Poems 1939–1962 Vol II*, copyright © 1944, 1948 by William Carlos Williams by permission of New Directions Publishing Corporation (US and Canadian rights).

All rights reserved. No paragraph of this publication may be reproduced, copied or transmitted save with written permission or in accordance with the provisions of the Copyright Act 1956 (as amended), or under the terms of any licence permitting limited copying issued by the Copyright Licensing Agency, 33-34 Alfred Place, London WC1E 7DP. Any person who does any unauthorised act in relation to this publication may be liable to criminal prosecution and civil claims for damages.

The right of Ben Knights to be identified as author of this work has been asserted by him in accordance with the Copyright, Designs and Patents Act 1988.

First published in the United Kingdom in 1995 by
Jessica Kingsley Publishers Ltd
116 Pentonville Road
London N1 9JB, England
and
1900 Frost Road, Suite 101
Bristol, PA 19007, U S A

Copyright © 1995 Ben Knights

Library of Congress Cataloging in Publication Data
A CIP catalogue record for this book is available from the Library of Congress

British Library Cataloguing in Publication Data
Knights, Ben
Listening Reader: Fiction and Poetry for
Counsellors and Psychotherapists
I. Title
801.95

ISBN 1-85302-266-7

Printed and Bound in Great Britain by
Athenaeum Press, Gateshead, Tyne and Wear

Contents

In memory of Margaret Dobie (Barnes)
(2 May 1923 – 6 April 1971)

Psychology would do better to turn directly to literature rather than to use it unawares.

(James Hillman, 1983, p.18)

What within myself, the reader may ask, what temperamental leanings, what view of the world, what standards, made it less or more easy for me to animate the world symbolised by the text? What hitherto-un-tapped potentialities for feeling, thought, and perhaps action, have I discovered through this experience? The possibilities are infinite: the insights derived from contrasts with my own temperament and my own environment; the empathy with violence, the sadistic impulse, that may now be faced and perhaps controlled: the compassion for others formerly felt to be alien; the opportunity for... 'ideal experimentation', that is, the trying out of alternative modes of behaviour in imagined situations...

(Louise Rosenblatt, 1978, pp.145–6)

'Tell me,' said Beloved, smiling a wide happy smile. 'Tell me your diamonds.'

> It became a way to feed her. Just as Denver discovered and relied on the delightful effect sweet things had on Beloved, Sethe learned the profound satisfaction Beloved got from storytelling. It amazed Sethe (a much as it pleased Beloved) because every mention of her past life hurt. Everything in it was painful or lost. She and Baby Suggs had agreed without saying so that it was unspeakable; to Denver's inquiries Sethe gave short replies or rambling incomplete reveries. Even with Paul D., who had shared some of it and to whom she could talk with a measure of calm, the hurt was always there...

> But, as she began telling about the earrings, she found herself wanting to, liking it. Perhaps it was Beloved's distance from the events itself, or her thirst for hearing it – in any case it was an unexpected pleasure.

(Toni Morrison, Beloved, p.58)

Preface

This book has been written out of the conviction that the kind of reading it advocates can be of profound significance to those whose occupations involve them in counselling, guidance or forms of psychotherapy – all those whose role includes practised listening. I am thinking especially of counsellors, social workers, clergy, probation officers, psychotherapists, and those responsible for their training and support. In the introduction I shall attempt to explain what this book is about, and to give an overview of its contents. I have to say first of all that I am a layperson in the fields I have just referred to, and that my own subject discipline is literature, though literature within the sphere of adult education, where teachers are always likely to be kept on their toes about the *uses* of their subject. In the last few years a good deal of interest has arisen in the threads that connect literary work with work on one sort or another of 'talking cure'. Recent teaching, conversations and books suggest to me that topics such as metaphor, symbolism, narrative, the constitutive power of language are again arousing interest on the part of those whose business is people. (Many of the books in this field are listed in the bibliography.)

Whether or not this book contributes to those debates, its main function is to act as a resource book, suggesting first some of the ways in which reading imaginative texts may feed into professional listening, and then providing examples in a way intended to help form connections. While its subject is not arts therapy as such, it does seek to tap the sources of creativity in the reader, sources which might then be more available in the therapeutic encounter. The therapist and the counsellor, I suppose, seek to help their clients towards adequate symbolisation. To do so, they themselves require access to a repertoire of modes of symbolisation. A full listening response itself includes the making up (overtly or in imagination) of empathic stories. This book seeks to be a medium for putting its readers in touch with forms of writing and the imaginative processes called out by that writing which may be of use to them.

Many people have helped with the making of this book, some of them without knowing it. I want to give special thanks for all their help and encouragement to Pamela Knights, Malcolm Sweeting, and Tim Bond. Also to Peter Cook, Jon Cook, Sue Habeshaw, Colin Evans, Jane Aaron, Nano MacCaughan, Barry Palmer, and all my other colleagues on the Development of University English

Teaching Project. I am grateful to all those who took part in the 'Healing Tests' courses at Durham, and to Jessica Kingsley and her staff. To go back further, many people were responsible for arousing my interest in the borderland between literary criticism and psychology. I would thus like to record how much I owe to my parents, Elizabeth and Lionel Knights, and (whether or not they realise what they did) to Denys Harding, and Jane Kitto. To another, my aunt, Margaret Dobie, the book is dedicated.

C.B.K.
Durham

But there are many *kinds* of knowledge, and it might be useful to make a provisional distinction between knowledge 'about' and empathic knowledge. The latter might be seen as knowledge in action. Flawed as this distinction may be, it suggests something of the kind of knowing with which reading a novel or watching a play provides us. The knowledge we engage with in books is at least in some respects similar to the knowledge we need to possess about people. It is knowledge immersed in practice, and not the least element in this is awareness of our own situation in the making of knowledge. As speakers or as listeners we are situated inside the occasions where meanings and knowledge are moulded into being. We are not just relays for truth (or for that matter falsehood), but collaborators in the attempt to tell meaningful stories. I do not simply toss my meanings at you and you do not simply toss yours back to me. The idea of dialogue is central to this book. Words, as Mikhail Bakhtin, the great linguist and exponent of dialogue, insists, are filled with the echoes of others' utterances.

One critique of counselling, therapy, and related practices has it that they are 'technologies of discourse', and that the therapeutic culture of the age represents the ever deeper infiltration of the self by the agencies of control and conformity. It is not an argument that those whose prestige depends upon that ethos ought to dismiss. There are certainly times when training seems to substantiate such suspicions. Thus the inventories, taxonomies, and diagrams which haunt training courses and manuals do in many ways appear to reduce humans, their emotions and relationships to mechanical and normative schemes. While such schemes are clearly useful as aids to awareness, they must, if they are not to become regulative, be complemented by other ways of putting things: ways of dramatising the human which emphasise process and which, by welcoming the unexpected, leave room for growth and change.

Any encounter between two or more persons can be seen in terms of what sociologists call reproduction (the affirmation and re-making of personal, inter-personal, or cultural norms), but also potentially as an occasion for change, for negotiation over what it means and what it could in the future mean to be human. The imperatives of dignity, justice, love have to be acknowledged and spoken before they can become the pretexts of structural change. Reading is one way of gaining experience of the making of meanings in all their overlapping contexts, deepening attention to how the potentials of human-ness can be explored and developed. In short, there is an important analogy between reading and listening, both of which can be more active processes than is commonly supposed. The deeper the inferential pool of which professional listeners can avail themselves, the wider their opportunity to facilitate the making of meanings. Fictions and poetry provide a laboratory of meaning in process.

The idea that human identity is not an essence, but is continually made and re-made through language, has fundamental implications for the disciplines of counselling and therapy. Without denying the reality of other forms of privation (economic, say, or emotional), I want also to point to the possibility of symbolic deprivation, the deprivation of forms of thinking and language through which people can name, and grasp what is happening to them. While this is a form of deprivation by no means confined to any single social class or group, it is also that form of deprivation which takes away the means to understand and therefore set about altering other injustices and inequalities. Communicative competence is quite as important as instrumental competence. This is not to say that everything would be OK if you could only talk about it. Rather, being OK or not being OK (and the actions OKness might necessitate) only become tangible on the basis of symbolic and discursive mobility. Adequate symbolisation is a precondition for purposive action. Summarising the work of Serge Leclaire (one of the French psycho-analysts who have seen the need to integrate psycho-analysis and language), Daniel Gunn (1988) speaks of psycho-analysis attempting to 'return the world and the body to desiring'.

> It seeks to do this through creation of a space in which patients can voice their own story for the first time: speak their becoming, and become in the space of their speaking... In the very non-identity of language and its referents, in language's non-present presence, a freedom and *a future* are, conditionally, to be found. (p.131)

We can find parallel thinking also within a more familiar idiom. Thus Harold Behr (1988) speaks of the essence of group analytic technique as lying in the 'promotion of a network of communication to counteract the effects of isolation', and goes on to say that the group

> absorbs the effect generated by her [the individual's] isolation and helps her to find the words with which to articulate it. Later, the individual discovers her own language. The inarticulate symptom has been rendered articulate, discharged, so to speak, into the common pool of group communication.[1] (p.309)

That common pool is the common pool of the group or of the dyad of counsellor and client. But the metaphor of the common pool is also one to which Winnicott found himself drawn in trying to locate cultural experience (Winnicott 1971, p.99). To put it another way, the cultural system which counsellors or therapists have themselves entered through their reading might become available to the sub-system engendered in the therapeutic encounter. In touch with a varied stock of scripts and types, the counsellor may be able to precede the client into a zone where it is safe to talk. If the counsellor is to assist in creating a space where it is safe to speak, he or she must have a secure footing in their own inner space, be capable of that 'intelligent subjectivity' which Christopher Bollas holds to be such an important part of the work of analysis (Bollas 1987, p.235). There is, it seems to me, an instructive parallel between the process of offering tentative

---

1   I am grateful to Nano MacCaughan for drawing my attention to this

interpretations and that 'loan of consciousness' of which in the domain of learning Vygostsky and his followers speak. If thought is internalised dialogue, then the dialogue within the therapeutic encounter provides a model for the thinking which follows. In turn, the quality of that dialogue is sustained by the therapist or counsellor's receptive capacity to draw upon a full and abundantly populated inner world.

The American critic and poet Kenneth Burke once spoke of literature as 'equipment for living'. Explaining what he meant, he went on to draw an analogy between fictions and proverbs. Proverbs, he argued, were attempts to 'name' recurrent situations and, in so naming them, give the speaker some power over them: they were 'strategies for dealing with situations'. Literature, he claimed (and it is not a claim that has always chimed with its study in Higher Education) was like that, only obviously longer and more involved. Nor need we restrict its function to labelling: the function of literature, says Jerome Bruner (1986)

> is to open us to dilemmas, to the hypothetical, to the range of possible worlds that a text can refer to. I have used the term 'to subjunctivize', to render the world less fixed, less banal, more susceptible to recreation. Literature subjunctivizes, makes strange, renders the obvious less so, the unknowable less so as well, matters of value more open to reason and intuition. Literature, in this spirit, is an instrument of freedom, lightness, imagination, and yes, reason. It is our only hope against the long gray night. (p.159)

In the same vein, the followers of Bakhtin think of the imaginative text as a 'prosthesis of the mind' (Holquist 1990). I propose that we may turn to literature as one source for languages in which to tell human experience. As I aim to show in the chapters which follow, we need to think of representations not simply as descriptive (this is what happened), but as productive. Our subject is the acquisition of a language for change, a language in which to frame situations and turn them into new situations. Tellings do not simply name that which already is – they are not simply retrospective – they name, and even bring about new possibilities. Literary texts have a particular usefulness here in being bounded. Their entailments to the world outside themselves are oblique: we can enter into imaginative play without fear of mistake. Misreading will have no direct consequences.

If all this sounds heavy-going, and as though solemnity is now to pursue you even into the recesses of the reading you might otherwise have engaged in for relaxation, this is because I have been labouring one part of my argument. There is another aspect to this advocacy of reading, and it does concern pleasure, a subject too easily associated in the professional mind with frivolity. Involvement with texts is a form of play, and a form of play that draws on the satisfactions of making, of giving shape, of bringing complexity into graspable form. Ordered words may be experienced with a charge of pleasure which carries us through the frustrating business of interpretation. We can read poems and novels in ways which foster our own creativity and unleash imaginative energies whose goal is not merely the re-arrangement of what we already know, but the discovery of what we did not know, had forgotten, or repressed. They give shape to what Bollas refers to as the 'unthought known', that which we at some level know but do not yet know how to articulate.

Since a good deal of the work of ideology is to induce amnesia, and since this social repression parallels and reinforces the work of repression within the individual, the task left to the artists may be (as Richard Webster (1990) has put it)

> that of repossessing the vast areas of the imagination and of society itself which have already been annexed by the forces of repression. Because the human imagination can never be ultimately confined, artists will always be free to join the forces of subversion in order to engage in such raids on the occupied territories of the mind. (p.62)

Unexpected images may provoke us as individuals or as citizens to draw on depths we have learned not to know we had.

Let me try to draw these threads together. I am suggesting that, attentively read, novels, plays, or poems, develop our empathy, our imagination, our repertoire of names for situations. Partly they do this through drawing on fantasies which have a more public currency than our own; and in acceding to a domain where fantasy is given public utterance we experience the re-alignment of our own compulsive mental norms and habits. In advancing the argument which follows I am drawing eclectically on literary theory, and in particular on those writers who have ushered in the 'return of the reader', the acknowledgement of the reader's share in making the patterns which he or she sees. I believe that reading can best be described as a dialogue between the codes on the page and the imagination, fantasy, memory, and skills of the reader. Our thought itself, says Bakhtin (1986), 'is born and shaped in the process of interaction and struggle with others' thought' (p.92). Neither side of this dialogue need be superior. Those who insist on dominating a dialogue in the end create boredom for themselves as well. Readers (like listeners) play their part in the making of sense, contributing to the evolution of forms in which complex experience may be held, thought, explored, and developed.

This book is laid out in the following way. It is divided into two parts, of which the first consists of theory and exposition, and the second of a practical guide to reading. Since what I go on to argue rests on an account of language, Chapter One clears some ground by synthesising relevant bits of recent linguistics and stylistics. Chapter Two gives a broad outline of the literary critical practices that seem most relevant to our topic, using a poem and a short story as its principal examples. In Chapter Three a more detailed case about poetry is made, and several examples are used to explore the kind of iconic and analogical thinking which poetry may enable. There are then two chapters which give further attention to two subjects which seem crucial to the argument, the subjects, respectively of metaphor and narrative. Chapter Six develops the thesis of the previous chapter in connection with fictional narratives. Chapter Seven takes the example of a specific short novel to demonstrate a mode of reading in action. The second part of the book consists first of an inventory of sample topics with suggested readings, and then of an annotated list of recommended authors. The book concludes with a bibliography of work which seems especially relevant to the borderland between literary study and applied psychology.

Part One

CHAPTER ONE

About Language

The thesis underlying this book is that listening and reading are interactive processes. Since meanings are made collaboratively, one role of the counsellor or therapist is to help create and sustain richer contexts of meaning. Consequently, some understanding of language and how language works is necessary to listeners and to readers. This chapter introduces ways of thinking about language which draw upon contemporary research and theory. These debates have very practical implications, and are thus not solely of interest to linguists and academic critics. I believe that without some awareness of such ways of thinking we are likely to be trapped within notions of language that limit in damaging ways our conception of what happens when we talk and write. Our failure to comprehend the nature of the relationships between speakers and listeners and of both to their language may have very practical consequences. I want to suggest that, paradoxically, we are both more dependent upon but also more creative in our use of language than people commonly suppose. I suggest that there are two basic misconceptions about language.

The first is that language has a straightforward, uncomplicated relationship to reality: according to this theory, there is a real world composed of unambiguous things and events. These things and events can be described in words, which thus provide a kind of transparent window between us and the world. We have experience, and subsequently express it in words. A thing and the word for it exist in a one-to-one relationship. The other misconception has to do with relations between speakers and listeners. Like the first, it is usually held tacitly, and is usually tied up with a notion of 'communication'. Language is a means of communication, the theory goes. Thoughts, ideas, information, knowledge generally, travel from A through the medium of language to B. Both theses have in common the notion that language is simply a channel, a medium through which something extra-linguistic is poured. They also have in common a kind of spurious neutrality. Language is a window: or, if it is a pipe, then any ineffective communication is simply a blockage to be removed by the nearest plumber or teacher of 'communication skills'. Further, in the communication thesis A and B

11

are visualised as equals – the nature of their relatedness, and issues of inequality of power or influence do not come into it. Communication, on this showing, is a matter of technique, and secondary, at all events, to the real stuff of life which is located in experience and in feeling. During the course of this chapter I shall dispute both these assumptions, and attempt to replace them with something more adequate.

In brief, my argument will be that language is a central form of human endeavour, not just a way of dressing up what already exists outside of language. Language is used for all sorts of purposes additional to the transfer of information from one head to another. It has its own history, rules, and habits which make it far more complex and obscure than we often imagine. I suspect this is intuitive knowledge for any one who has ever struggled to say or write anything difficult, but it is also a knowledge that communication mongers constantly obscure. There are formidable and well-funded forces in a society like ours bent on insisting that everything is really very simple and can be expressed very simply (in ways that suit their interests). But as the protagonist of Harold Brodkey's novel *The Runaway Soul* remarks in one of his less narcissistically absorbed moments, things 'are simple because of short sentences, not because of anything in life'. If the soundbite syndrome has enough in common with 'common sense' to conceal the inherent complexity of things, it also makes it appear that language is innocuous, uncontaminated by power and influence. Actually, language has its roots deep in the social structure as well as in the individual psyche. Its field of effect is social through and through. While we cannot take on these subjects at any length here, this chapter will be informed by such arguments.

This chapter starts with the notion of 'signs' and 'signifiers', and the way in which languages pervade social life. Since the underlying notion is that language is constitutive rather than merely descriptive (we make realities as we talk them) I then go on to investigate how language may be said to create the thinkable, looking at language as a system for classifying and connecting, and introducing the dimensions of lexis and syntax. This leads to the notion of style and choices – the interdependence of what is said with how it is said. From there we go on to survey some of the things language does in addition to its referential function. That will compel some attention to matters of relationships and the pragmatic dimension of language. Finally, I examine the levels at which language operates, the idea of multiple meaning, and ambiguity which gives rise to the need for interpretation. Throughout, examples will be included which will, I hope, be of interest to those who work in counselling and therapy.

SIGNS AND SIGNIFICATION

Let us begin with 'signs'. The theory of signs (often referred to as 'semiology' or 'semiotics') holds that almost everything humans make – perhaps everything – can be read as a language. (We shall return shortly to the relevance of all this to language in the more usual sense.) The sign, in this tradition, is held to be composed of two elements: the 'signified' which is an idea, a mental construct, and the 'signifier' which is a material event or object, a sound, a word, a drawing, a mark on paper. Signifiers allude to signifieds in a number of possible ways. Some are 'iconic': they look to some degree like the object they represent (photographs, naturalistic statues). Others are 'unmotivated': the connection between the signifier and the signified is in a formal, although not an historical, sense arbitrary (usually, although not invariably, the case with linguistic signs). Signification takes place at 'denotative' and 'connotative' levels. Denotation is, so to speak, the simplest level of meaning: a logo of a little crown on an envelope may simply be a picture of a crown. Things get more interesting (and more plausible) as we move to the level of connotation: the emblem of the crown stands for the monarch, and thus for the British government. Any trivial bureaucratic communication may be dignified in this way. Behind my letter from the tax inspector, it reminds me, lurks the whole apparatus of the British state.

Advertising has provided a field day for the critical reader of signs. Thus to seize an example from an infinite supply, the glossy photograph of a country scene may at one level simply be a picture of a country scene. But the cultural code 'countryside' leads us to read that picture as an allusion to naturalness, the desirability of the country over the city, the longing for the good life, and an idyllic 'England'. The qualities that we recognise in the picture are thus imputed to the product. Likewise, human activities (dressing, eating, sitting, getting about) can be read as statements about status, or states of mind, gender relations, attitudes, or beliefs.

This approach – treating language as the central social performance – has permitted the reading of food, fashion, cars, clothing, furnishings, physical posture, and so on, as languages, often with highly illuminating results. (Incidentally, the subject of 'body language' represents a psychological adaptation of this widespread preoccupation with sign systems.) The drawback is that if everything is a language, to what do any of these 'signifying practices' refer? Why, to another language. There is a dizzying tendency on the part of those who profess semiotics to demonstrate that any signified, closely observed, is just another signifier in an apparently unending sequence. This play of languages is what in recent years the philosophy of 'deconstruction' has been built upon. There has been a tendency for some theorists to sound (maddeningly enough for common sense) as though there were no referents outside language, and thus on occasion the practice of linguistic theory has sounded oddly akin to the philosophic tradition known as 'idealism': the belief that since what we know are concepts and ideas, not things, we could have no evidence of what the realm of things was like or even whether it existed at all. Far-fetched as all this may sound, it has something rather important to say.

LANGUAGE AT WORK

One of the key doctrines of semiotics is what has been known as the arbitrary nature of the sign. By this is meant that representations have a conventional rather than a natural connection with the thing they purport to represent. A doodle of a cat only 'looks like' a cat because there is a convention (a tacit social agreement) that you can depict cats as a smaller circle on top of a larger one, with two little triangles for ears, another line for a tail, all bounded by wiry lines. There is a good deal of argument about the degree to which signs are arbitrary, and as suggested above, some signifiers are plainly more motivated than others. Yet the thesis has a use, which I shall try to illustrate by reverting to language in the more traditional sense. Here too the linguistic sign is held to be arbitrary. This does not mean that you just give names to things at whim, depending on how you are feeling that morning. Nor does it mean that words are without history. (Although, in point of fact, the linguistics from which all this is derived, the work of Ferdinand de Saussure, *was* an attempt to break away from the great nineteenth-century tradition of historical philology.) But the theory does point to the degree to which convention rules in assigning labels to things and events, and it thus provides a corrective to our tendency to regard the identity between words and the things they label as natural. The linguistics derived from Saussure views language as a system of oppositions, where the meaning of terms derives not from any inherent affinity between signifier and referent but is established by contrast, typically in a binary set. Thus the idea of 'normality' only exists in relation to 'abnormality', 'adult' in relation to 'child', 'male' to 'female', 'natural' in contrast to 'artificial' and so on. Even 'natural' things are affected by the way we classify them in language.

Language plays a major part in shaping attitudes and belief, and language is not neutral. One procedure of the powerful is always to impose definitions which have the effect of neutralising phenomena or rendering them harmless. It is not insignificant that the department of state which deals with military matters is called the Ministry of Defence. The Gulf War brought back the term 'collateral damage' as a euphemism for civilian casualties. Or think of the emotional emptiness of such employment terms as 'redundancy' or 'wastage'. By the same token, those who are engaged in struggle with the status quo often seek to exercise their own power over definitions: one thinks of the success of re-naming the community charge the 'poll tax', or the immense linguistic work carried out by feminism.

Some would argue that our perception and thinking is so permeated by language that all our thinking is shaped by what language permits us to say. We cannot think our way out of language. It is doubtful whether this proposition could ever be proved one way or the other (although there is evidence that some thinking at least is pre- or even non-linguistic). It also begs important questions about where change would come from, or who influences linguistic choices. I would prefer to say that language acts to organise and stabilise our perceptions: where we have a word or a manner of saying things, we are inclined to assume the existence of a clear, discrete reality as a referent. Language has social knowledge built into it, and the effect of repetition is always to normalise. As I have suggested, this is the case even in connection with the 'natural' world, which would appear to be a domain of pretty solid and unarguable objects. Even here, the classificatory propensity of language can be seen to fashion the real. We might say that we notice the things we have words for – language elaborates and reinforces the perceptual grids through which we filter even 'natural' objects. You do not 'see' a landscape unless you are culturally predisposed to perceive a visual field containing hills, streams, woods, and farms in a particular way (for example as uplifting, or therapeutic, or beautiful). And just as you see a view through the lens of innumerable photographs and paintings and postcards emulating paintings, so you see (shall we say) 'girls and boys' through the lens of learned presuppositions. We *learn* to see as we do, and language is a major element in that learning. One classic example linguists sometimes use is the colour spectrum, a physical continuity segmented into discrete colours by linguistic terms. Our sense of a world made up of separate objects, self-contained within their own boundaries is a linguistic construct.

What I am saying about the classification of things by language is even more the case when we come to social and psychological realities. Here, once again, language does not simply encode pre-existing methods of looking at the world: it actively creates and organises them. To take an example from the realm of geopolitics, the binary set East/West does, of course, reflect certain political realities, but it also *is* one of those realities, a standing invitation to policy makers, weapons manufacturers, and the public at large to think of the world in those terms. If we organise what we know about the world in East/West terms, we are asserting the importance of some facts about the world over others. Things that do not fit in with our model will become invisible. Furthermore, because of our tendency to naturalise language, we will tend to make the (usually unconscious) assumption that where there is a word there must be a thing to correspond to it. 'East' and 'West' cease to represent provisional and inadequate stabs at describing reality, and come to be seen as corresponding to absolute truth. Where we have a label, we adopt behaviour appropriate to that label.

This back formation from word to reality is especially striking in the everyday social world, as also in the domain of emotions and inner experience. If we have a term such as 'youth' or 'teenager' we assume a reality corresponding to what is indicated by those words. The definition is self-reinforcing, since the behaviour of those so labelled can be accounted for in terms of the supposed essence of teenagerhood, or youthdom. Since labels are often used as though they were explanations, the procedure becomes circular. Or if we think of emotions, our perceptions of mental states congregate around the term we have available. Words like 'depression' or 'anxiety' organise (give shape and meaning to) all sorts of more or less nebulous conditions, and may well offer some relief by giving a frightening and amorphous state a name. This gives us some sense of control over it, and aligns it with what other people have experienced. Even terms such as 'state', 'emotion', 'feeling' and so on, of which we all avail ourselves, imply the existence of solid, discrete entities. Indeed, we tend to think of words themselves as solid, tangible entities, a habit doubtless fostered by the appearance and permanence of the written word. Even the highly perishable spoken word (the beginning of the word 'perishable' has vanished into silence long before I have finished saying it) comes to be thought of as a solid object. We find it reassuring to postulate a constant essence 'behind' all its individual manifestations.

The gendering of language provides a wealth of examples of how constitutive and normative functions work. Feminists have rightly pointed out the way in which the generic use of 'man' and of the masculine pronoun reinforces beliefs that agents are normally male. Equally, there are far more belittling and degrading words for women than there are for men. Even the (apparently) harmless habit of referring to a young woman as a girl has the effect of framing her as young and in need of parental supervision. But, once again, feminism, like other movements of liberation, reminds us that language is a field of negotiation and contest. We need not be entirely at the mercy of the definitions imposed upon us.

ABOUT STYLE

While this chapter is not intended as a tract on contemporary linguistics, my contention that some understanding of language is necessary to professional listeners does necessitate carrying the excursion a little further. So far I have only talked in terms of language giving labels, organising the world of things and events by giving us handles by which to know them. The time has come to sketch in some categories with which to classify and organise the undifferentiated rush of language in use. The merest outline has to suffice. I shall therefore simplify an available model and speak of language as existing in two dimensions, sometimes spatialised by being drawn as the two axes of a graph. It will be obvious that this is simply a way of carving up and rendering thinkable a dynamic and ever-moving phenomenon. And the two axes I refer to are in permanent and necessary relation to each other, can indeed only be realised through each other. If we work with this mental map, our vertical (paradigmatic) axis may be visualised as having to do with the choice of individual words, everything known to linguists as *lexis* and to non-specialists as vocabulary – the almost infinite range of words that could be used. Our horizontal (syntagmatic) axis alludes to the production of words in time and concerns *syntax* (grammar), the elaborate system of rules according to which words are connected with each other to form utterances which native speakers of the language can recognise, even if they have never thought of uttering them themselves. Although language is bound to operate in time, it is useful to imagine it as exhibiting these two dimensions, with the slots in the syntactic chain being filled by a vast range of possible words and still making sense. To tie this point to our general theme: I am saying that we need to attend not only to the words people choose, but the manner in which they connect those words together. Not, as it were, to mark them for correct or incorrect grammar (contemporary linguistics are descriptive, not prescriptive) but as a way of listening out for the mental world behind the formulation.

Much of what has been said so far implies that humans are bound by their language, and indeed there is much in the prevalent philosophical systems of the last thirty years to support linguistic determinism. As children learn their language they simultaneously learn the values of their culture. Can you think your way out of the linguistic arrangements you have learned? No one can fabricate totally new utterances: we have to work within the grammatical limits of our language, of which we have learned the basic rules by the age of four. Certain beliefs about the status of objects, about transitivity, and causation are very deeply laid down. However, the basic rules still allow an infinity of possible utterances: in any case linguistic determinism is vulnerable to the same criticisms as any other determinism. There are even some grounds for linguistic optimism. For one thing, language can and does change, both in terms of its lexical options, and also (more slowly) in terms of its syntax. As pointed out above, radical movements have generally seen one of their objects as the re-making of linguistic habits. Second, within the basic framework of the language it is possible to make a very large number of choices about what you say and how you say it. 'She appeared to be somewhat irritable', 'she lost her temper repeatedly' and 'she was in a fucking awful mood' are all possible English utterances, and may describe the same occasion. So too may 'The file in question appears to have been accidentally mislaid', and 'I've lost the sodding thing'. But as utterances they each have a rather different ring, and are redolent of different contexts of report. We cannot in fact avoid the subject of style. A style (that is to say a characteristic pattern of usage) is a means for thinking the world.

In analysing style we are here concerned as much with the diagnostic use of what people and texts say as a guide to their thought processes as with the way language shapes thought. While the language sets outer limits to the sayable and influences us in the direction of saying some things rather than others, there is still a good deal of choice available to the individual speaker or writer. It is a matter of listening to how people put things as well as to the content of what they say; being receptive to style as the outward expression of thought processes. Our key notion here is that *how* something is said is as important as *what* is said. Much of the drift of textual studies in this century has been informed by the perception that form (the how) is inextricably bound up with content (the what).

A few examples may serve to make the necessary connections between the domain of speech and listening and that of writing and reading.

The propensity noted above to turn acts and fluid phenomena into solid imaginary entities leads us directly to what some linguists call 'nominalisation'. This term has its origins in transformational grammar, but I shall gloss it simply as the tendency to turn what we might expect to meet as a verb into a noun or noun phrase: 'The propensity noted above', 'my impression is' or 'the police action came at the end of a day when...' This particular stylistic habit is prevalent in the field of talk about emotions and feelings, where it encourages the belief that behaviours which we might (using an alternative grid) see as activities or acts of persons are conditions or subjects in their own right, independent of the person whom they effect. 'He has an alcohol problem', 'I was gripped by terror', or 'her irritation was obvious' propose in their different ways that an alcohol problem, terror, or irritation are separate and autonomous phenomena. Which may well be what they sometimes feel like. The point is once again that we can easily be misled by language into the realistic fallacy I referred to above: to suppose that the utterance names a fixed reality behind the words. Words, I suggest, always represent an attempt to get at significance rather than a parade of fixed and unambiguous meanings.

Different utterances (even when they concern the same subject matter) foreground different aspects of the same situation, and – by the same token – background others. 'I suffer from depression', and 'I sometimes get depressed' may appear to be essentially the same statement, but each connotes a slightly different stance. Nominalisation (like the use of the passive) is apt to site the subject in a universe under the control of forces outside the self. While this may be an accurate reflection of historical reality, it is a hopeless basis for realising such autonomy as we may have room for. The presumption of independent forces over which the self has no control helps to create the condition to which it alludes. 'He has an alcohol problem' conceptualises matters in a very different way from 'he drinks too much', and a therapist might well use linguistic reframing to move towards achieving the goal of heightened self-responsibility (a point developed in different ways by both Paul Watzlawick (1978) and Dorothy Rowe (1987)).

Nominalisation is akin to another tendency of thought, and one which will surface again in discussions of role and figure in narrative. This is the learned reflex by which we collapse act into actor, suggesting as we do so that we can name an individual's essence (thus some one who cleans offices for a living is likely to be referred to as 'a cleaner', and some one who has committed a crime as 'a criminal'). Linguistic habits shape attitudes.

The examples represent only a sample from the vast range of possibilities, but they do indicate important areas. All I can hope to do here is to give some indication of the kind of linguistic phenomena one might look out for, and suggest how style works in two directions: as indicative of the thought processes of the speaker, and as representing the thought processes being urged upon the listener or reader. In a narrow logic, passive statements ('the children have been fed', 'I was told to come here') are the same as active statements, since they have the same propositional content ('he fed the children', 'someone told me to come'). Rhetorically, and stylistically they are not the same. Repeated use of the passive where the active would be possible builds up a sense of a world where things happen to the grammatical subject rather than the subject doing things itself. Furthermore, the use of the passive permits 'agent deletion', which is to say it allows you to leave out or evade the matter of *who* did it. This may be because the speaker does not actually know who did it ('plans have been made'; 'it has been said that...'). However, the repeated absence of agents builds up a picture of a world where things just happen, apparently without the intervention of active subjects ('twenty people were arrested', 'a compromise has been agreed'). There may be real fudge about who did it, and a displacement of attention from cause to victim. Repeated use of the passive pushes away questions about agency, and suggests that the speaker occupies a world where things are done to you, things over which you have little or no control.

If we are thinking about the relation between what people say and the mind style of the speaker, it seems unavoidable to say something about a whole bundle of things having to do with the relations between the various elements of a sentence. Once again, this is a vast and complex field, to which there is only space to offer a few pointers. Basically, the syntax of any sentence (as a gross simplification, let us treat language as composed of sentences) enacts presuppositions about states, processes, and actions – what kind of process is attributable to what kind of entity, and who may be expected to do what and to whom. Some sentences tell us about states ('he's a weak man'), some about actions ('she's coming home for Christmas'), others about processes ('I'm learning to do without it'). One very important formation is that in which an agent performs an intentional action which leads to a change of state in an object ('I threw him out of the house'). Such sentences contrast with intransitives where a process takes place without a grammatical object ('nothing is happening'; 'she's grown a lot'). However, many sentences raise expectations of full transitivity, but do not fulfil them. They may, for example, suggest that the doing is done by something inanimate ('the car is destroying the environment'). Or they may propose abstract entities as predicates ('another week like that will drive me mad'; 'house prices are forcing many people to move out of the area'; 'greed is responsible for most of the world's ills'). We might also note those occasions on which an action is attributed to an inanimate subject that would normally be attributed to an animate one ('The clutch screamed'; 'my back's killing me'; 'life has given her a raw deal'). Attention to these matters is important because recurrent usage both tells us something about the way people think, and appeals to us to think likewise. If someone says 'he makes me sick', their way of putting it attributes the cause of their feeling to another person. Different kinds of transitivity may denote a world of human choices and actions, or a world governed by impersonal forces over which we have no control.

My last example in this lightning tour of stylistics concerns a phenomenon sometimes known as 'modalisation'. We make the useful assumption that an utterance can be divided up into different levels, in this instance those of 'proposition' and 'modality'. Proposition alludes to the conceptual content of an utterance; modality to the speaker's attitude towards that content, and also (fascinatingly for our purposes) to their attitude to their audience. Included here is the phenomenon of 'hedging' – avoiding committing yourself to a definite statement. A simple proposition like 'he is lonely' can be modalised in a number of different ways. Thus it could become a question 'is he lonely?', or coloured with uncertainty ('I think he's lonely'/'He seems to be lonely') or hesitancy ('Er, I think, I mean it seems to me anyway, he's um lonely'). This distinction between proposition and modality enables us to perceptualise statements in the light of the speaker's attitude, both towards what they say and and towards the person(s) to whom they say it. Thus recurrent hesitancy phenomena are likely to encode the speaker's diffidence, their unsureness about what they know and whether they have a right to tell their listener anything. Such modalisation may well be an indicator of perceived inequality in the setting in which it occurs. Someone who keeps linguistically covering their tracks may be coding their own sense of occupying a lower status and consequently less privileged access to knowledge than the person to whom they are speaking. Such characteristics may also be one mechanism by which transferences are conveyed. The topic makes a useful bridge to the next section.

INTERPERSONAL FEATURES OF LANGUAGE

Language, I have been arguing, is productive. It follows that through language we simultaneously make meanings and manage relationships. Speaking or writing are not simply the expression of experience but actions in themselves. By analogy, people in a group who sigh, yawn loudly or belch are not necessarily just responding to physiological need (there is a language of yawning). I spoke earlier of language as involving not only statements about 'realities', but also relationships between speakers and listeners, writers and readers. To these relationships I now return. Let us focus on the relational dimension of language, and on language as a means of doing things in the world. As the proponents of 'speech act theory' have pointed out, many linguistic acts can be regarded as actions in their own right (promising, threatening, persuading...). Let me start with a triangle composed of reality – speaker – listener. In this referential model, the speaker communicates propositions about reality to a listener. This is fine so far as it goes, but it leaves out the effects of the interpersonal dimension (it also leaves out the dialogic interchange between speaker and listener roles, but we may by-pass that for the moment). It implies, that is, what I earlier called a 'spurious neutrality' about the communicative act. It is true that most utterances are to some degree referential – they allude to a referent outside themselves – but utterances have other features as well, and prime among these is the function of persuasion.

When we say things, we are not simply making dispassionate observations about the world. We are actively (and often covertly) trying to persuade our listener both that what we have to say is worth listening to, and that our view of things is the correct one. If you come home from work and say to your partner 'I've had about enough of that wretched man', you are not simply making a factual statement about a situation, you are also asserting the correctness of your version of events, and inviting your partner to take sides with you against that monster – a minor example, but then linguistic life is made up of countless small examples which cumulatively become persuasive. At another level of discourse, a politician who informs us that 'there is no alternative', or 'the tide is turning against the government' is engaged in persuasion decked out as the neutral description of reality. The subtext tries to create the reality it talks about by enlisting us on the speaker's side.

We are probably aware, if we stop to think about it, that we frequently use language for purposes other than disinterested reference. A common example is the so-called 'phatic' use of language, where we are checking the presence of a communicative circuit, as when strangers first get into conversation. It is unlikely that conversational offerings about the weather bring much in the way of new information to either party , but they do establish the possibility of getting into conversation, and an ambience of friendliness. Controversial topics are normally avoided on such occasions. My broader point is that, more generally, language acts take place in specific contexts, and that the social dimension of the context bears directly upon what gets said. In fact, there is a pretty exact analogy between this interpersonal dimension of language and the existence of maintenance roles in a group. Just as a group will need to work at maintenance as well as task, so in language people are managing and servicing relations at the same time as speaking referentially about content. We are here moving towards the notion of discourse, that is to say language as social practice. Social psychologists of language point out that identities, norms, and attitudes are constructed and reconstructed in the course of linguistic interaction. Discourse is oriented not solely towards 'truth', but towards the person addressed. That person will in turn understand what they have heard in the light of the context they share with the speaker. There can be little doubt that the circumstances of the counselling session itself call out particular modes of speaking and interacting.

In referring to the persuasive dimension of language I am drawing attention to the way in which speech is always oriented towards a goal. It is highly relevant for those engaged upon developing the arts of listening to recognise that dimension of speech which involves persuading your interlocutor of the validity of your position, and inviting them into complicity with you. Struggle as we may to achieve a disinterested account of reality, the likelihood is that all utterances will embody a persuasive function. Utterances, points out Bakhtin (1986), 'are not indifferent to each other, and are not self-sufficient; they are aware of and mutually reflect each other... Each utterance refutes, affirms, supplements, and relies on the others...' (p.91). We have to understand utterances as embodying stance and as in some degree rhetorical, their propositional content pointed up or emphasised in the interests of persuasion. Statements such as 'the 'phone hasn't stopped ringing all morning', or 'I turned up, but there was nobody else around', or 'no one wears those any more' *could* be literally true, but more likely they (a) express the speaker's feelings about events, and (b) seek solidarity with the hearer on a basis of sympathy and partisanship. Everyday speech is full of rhetorical devices used to enhance bare statements by giving them interlocutive force. Exaggeration (as in the examples cited above) is prominent among these. Other examples include irony – 'the one day I managed to come home early he wasn't even back himself'; 'the moment I got the washing out it started to rain', and its more militant versions, often signalled by 'of course': 'of course, they never even came round to look'. The speaker indicates his/her attitude to 'them' and incites the listener to join in. Or again, we might note the rhetorical force of pronouns, like the academic/pedagogic force of the 'we' I have just used, which implies membership of a joint enterprise, or the politician's 'we' (naturally you want to identify with all right thinking people).

In all these instances I am drawing attention to interpersonal features of language which are subject to more or less conscious control on the part of the speaker. While we cannot here take on the whole vast field of sociolinguistics, I ought at least to point out that language does not simply occur between completely free parties to the exchange, but within specific and constraining social contexts. This is the field of dialect; all those variations of vocabulary, syntax, pronunciation, and intonation that characterise different regional and socio-economic groups. The reason for alluding to this vast field here is to remind that parties to a linguistic transaction will often quite unconsciously be demonstrating allegiances that bear upon what is said, and, crucially, upon the relationship between them as speakers. This is especially true in a culture such as that of Britain, where regional and educational differences are inextricably tied up with issues of class and status: a conversation apparently about something else may well be indirectly re-enacting a long history of the 'hidden injuries of class'. Persistent use of abstract nouns, impersonal forms, and elaborate syntax coupled with 'received pronunciation' will code 'education' and hence higher status in many contexts, even if the speaker is completely unaware of their effect. It is likely that many encounters between (say) social workers and clients, doctors and patients, or teachers and parents are fissured by social barriers encoded in language usage.

Relevant for our purposes, too, is the concept of 'register'. 'Register' refers to the differing varieties of speech someone may command in different situations. Unconsciously, that is to say, we weigh up contexts, and slip into a different linguistic gear, playing up or down our natural accent, choosing more or less unusual words, producing more or less complex sentences, opting for or excluding slang, or swear words. Thus the language of children in the playground will tend to differ from their language in the classroom, and both from their language at home. Adults, too, are likely to use a different register among their friends from that they would use in a formal situation such as an interview. Most people make intuitive summings up of situations, and opt for what they sense to be the appropriate register for the occasion. This observation has important consequences: for one thing it draws attention to people's linguistic range (you are not necessarily stuck in the same style of speech all the time). For another, it opens up to investigation matters of why people speak as they do in the here and now: to what in *this* setting are they responding? Why is she being hyper-careful with her choice of words? why is she suddenly speaking 'estuary English'? or why is he lacing what he says with sexual innuendo? In language we process relationships and subject matter simultaneously.

LEVELS OF MEANING

Implicit throughout this chapter has been the notion that language operates on a number of different levels. In any given linguistic transaction, several of these levels may be simultaneously present. From the perspective of the listener or reader, one of our tasks is to listen out for all the things that may be simultaneously going on in an utterance. The last part of this chapter concerns the idea of multiple meaning, and the clues to look out for in working out what is being said. This subject leads us directly to the work with texts promised by the book as a whole. It will surely come as no surprise to professional listeners that meaning works on a number of different levels at once; that someone speaking may be saying something about a particular topic, alluding to their relationship to that subject, and their relationship to their listener all at the same time. To this we might add that even an apparently straightforward proposition is usually capable of being heard or read in more than one way. In everyday life we devote a lot of effort to trying to establish what people mean by what they say, even if the surface meaning was obvious. This potential for multiple meaning necessitates the interpretative activity which constitutes the subject matter of this book as well as the focus of therapy and counselling.

Perhaps the best place to get hold of this would be to revert to something I said about signs and signification earlier in this chapter. There I pointed out that there were different levels or orders of signification. One way of conceptualising this was to talk about 'denotation' and 'connotation'. Denotation was, so to speak, the straightforward, dictionary meaning of a word or phrase; connotation that

GARNETT LIBRARY

SMSU-WEST PLAINS

cloud of associations, and other meanings a word or concept will develop. Connotation leads us on to the subject of metaphor which will be discussd later on. Here, it is enough to say that even what appear on the surface to be statements of measurable fact generally resonate with further meanings. 'It's getting very late' or 'I can't get hold of it' may not simply be statements about time or physical grip. We are faced with a version of the Freudian distinction between manifest and latent meaning. Listeners, like readers, are called upon to decode what they hear in order to grasp the full implications of what is said. There *are* examples of kinds of discourse which function at one level only, where the leap to further implication is blocked off. An example would be technical manuals such as those which propose to tell you how to service your car, or a leaflet on how to assemble a flat-pack wardrobe. Texts of this kind can – ideally – be read in one way and one way only. But such texts are much less common than we tend to think – implication, additional meaning, is the rule rather than the exception. This means that the role of the listener or reader is much more complex than it would be if we could simply decode utterances by running them through a mental pro-gramme which would straightforwardly convert script or sound into meaning. There will be much to say later of the need for the listener to tolerate ambiguity and hold meaning in the making.

One corollary of what I have been saying leads us to 'symbolism'. It is difficult to define symbolism adequately, especially since we have recognised that any signifier is, strictly, a symbol (it is a representation of the thing it alludes to, not the thing itself). Language is characterised by its capacity for displacement, for recalling things not physically present. By 'symbol' I refer here to the idea that an object or event is likely to be endowed with meaning beyond the obvious surface meaning. Humans tend to charge the tangible world with meanings that go far beyond immediate material value. Preparing, giving, and receiving food, opening and closing doors, entering or leaving a group are deeply symbolic acts as well as physical ones. As we push towards the further levels of what is said to us it is this dimension of symbolism that opens up.

Symbolism may be cultural, or it may be idiosyncratic, local to an individual or a family (roses, in western culture, symbolise sexual passion; the cross has almost inescapable symbolic weighting). Usually, symbolism will move between the two poles: so individuals will attach their own meanings to their gardens, yet the meanings they attach will have potency within a set of cultural understandings about what gardens are and what they are for. Listeners, like readers, must attune themselves to the symbolism (the potential for other meanings) of the things to which speakers refer. We are all broadly aware of this. We are apt to recognise that, say, the purchase of a BMW, or a fitted kitchen, or the biggest freezer in the neighbourhood is coded. We speak, or used to, of 'status symbols', and 'sex symbols'. When we turn to literary texts we shall see how the repetition of an item or motif tends to accrete meaning. And what I have said here about the symbolism of objects applies equally to the symbolic meaning of events.

In the introduction I spoke of the return of the reader, the growing acknow-ledgement in literary studies of the active part played by the reader in constructing meanings. The thesis has powerful applications to the role of the listener as well, for the corollary is that the act of listening requires a complex attention to all that we could describe (metaphorically) as lying behind, in between, or beneath the words. As we listen, we are constructing the speaker's universe (or how it appears to us that the universe appears to them) by an elaborate if largely intuitive inference, from the style as well as the content of what they say. Those whose training has focused on listening and interpretation will already be well aware that listening is an activity. I believe that the activity of the skilled listener and that recommended by theorists of reading may turn out to have exciting points of convergence and reinforcement. Both gain from being based upon a theory of language as the dynamic making of meanings in social contexts.

SUGGESTIONS FOR FURTHER READING

David Crystal (ed) (1987) *The Cambridge Encyclopedia of Language.* Cambridge: Cambridge UP.

Jonathan Culler, *Barthes* (1983) and *Saussure* (1976) in Fontana Modern Masters Series.

Norman Fairclough (1989) *Language and Power.* Harlow: Longman.

Roger Fowler (1981) *Literature as Social Discourse.* London: Batsford.

Roger Fowler (1986) *Linguistic Criticism.* Oxford: Oxford UP.

Howard Giles and Nikolas Coupland (1991) *Language: Contexts and Consequences.* Buckingham: Open UP.

Terence Hawkes (1977) *Structuralism and Semiotics.* London: Methuen.

Robert Hodge and Gunther Kress (1979) *Language as Ideology.* London: Routledge.

Robert Hodge and Gunther Kress (1988) *Social Semiotics.* Cambridge: Polity.

Dale Spender (1980) *Man Made Language.* London: Routledge.

Rosemary J. Stevenson (1993) *Language, Thought and Representation.* Chichester: John Wiley.

Deborah Tannen (1990) *You Just Don't Understand: Women and Men in Conversation.* London: Virago.

CHAPTER TWO

The Uses of Fiction

The previous chapter elaborated the argument that the making of meanings was a social and transactive process. Similarly, we might argue that reading is not simply the transfer of information from one head to another, but a constructive activity. In this chapter we are going to take a closer look at the dialogue between the reader and the text, and sketch in some of the ways in which we might characterise and value literary reading. All reading is constructive, as readers use their knowledge of the language and the conventions of reading and of the genre of text to decipher what they see before them. Some readings may, however, be more constructive than others, or rather, to formulate the point more sharply, certain kinds of text are better camouflaged than others, coming to us claiming an innocent transparency ('I speak the truth about the world; that is just how things *are*'), while others draw more attention to their own artifice.

I propose that a literary text invites the reader into co-production: that until the reader's mind gets to work on it, it is merely a mass of paper, glue and printer's ink, its meanings latent and unrealised. The reader's activity is analogous to the work of a drama company which takes a playscript and turns it into a play. Readers perform the work in their heads. Even the simplest utterance requires the listener to go beyond the information given. So at a slightly higher level of complexity, if I say 'It was one of those blue days on the east coast when you can taste the sunlight through the sharp air, and the wind is full of crying gulls and empty crisp packets', the chances are that even if you have never been to Skegness or Whitby you visualise a scene. You fill in the gaps from your own inferential stock. If it were the opening of a novel (it isn't) you would continue on the basis of amazingly few linguistic cues to create characters, situations, scenes out of the stuff of memory and fantasy. Even at the most basic level of the text's 'existents' (its freight of simulated characters, places, objects) most of what appears to be there is put there by your mind. The reader actualises what is only implicit. Like the listener, the reader is engaged in an activity of putting together clues: filling in gaps, making hypotheses, filling in contexts in which utterances might make sense, struggling to achieve coherence. At a more sophisticated level, you enter into dialogue with the text over the meaning of what happens, and try to sort out why in any case you are being addressed like this. Is this an ice cream advertisement? What are you as reader expected to do next? You do not as reader have completely free rein – the text is not like an inkblot into which you can read whatever you fancy. But at the same time it is not a jug which pours a set of complete, fixed meanings into your head.

Central to this book is the idea that we do not possess a fixed stock of mental schema with which to carry out the work of inference and understanding. It is through language and culture that humans as a species have created themselves. Literary reading – the attentive reading of poems and fictions of all sorts – is a way of adding to our inferential resources, elaborating and extending our stock of schema, the scripts and types we use to make sense of what we hear and thus in turn to make sense of events and persons. Let us take a closer look at the nature of the activity which I am advocating.

I am talking about reading literary texts (plays, poems, novels, and so on), but reading them in such a way as to maximise our engagement with them. Later, we will have to come back to what we might mean by a literary text. Here, let's take the easy way out, and assume that it is a text which is read in a particular way. Part of my claim is that the bounded nature of texts facilitates moving around within them, cross-referencing and thinking things through. Since many of the entailments to the outside world are cut, there will be no practical consequences if we get things wrong. Further, in a world where language written and spoken pours at us all day, and where we learn to read fast as a matter of survival, the act of deliberately slowing down our reading of certain items is (while difficult) profoundly educative. It forces us to confront things about texts and our relations to their form and content that we might otherwise overlook. In addition, there are statements worth dwelling on, coming back to and re-thinking. We might call this impeded reading; a way of reading which (whether by virtue of the obstacles presented by the text or as a result of our own self-discipline) broods reflectively upon the words.

By itself, reading slowly is probably not enough to enable us to unpack layers of meaning. We need to draw upon the repertoire of the formal study of literature, drawing out from it those aspects that are of most use for our present purposes, and it is those which this and the following chapters aim to explore. The criterion of relevance to the task in hand means that I shall have little to say about a major area of literary study – context and history. While we need to acknowledge and allow for historical and cultural difference, the time available to readers of this book will probably preclude them from much reading around the text. Ideally, a reading needs to be enhanced by paying attention to the historical context from which a text emerges, the language and conventions of its time, questions of social history, of the biography of the author, the history of publishing and of audiences. For present purposes, we will put aside most of these things. This leaves us with a clump of activities which together comprise literary criticism. They are probably most easily visualised as a triad in which each pole interlinks with the others, but may be emphasised in its own right.

The poles of this triad I shall call description, interpretation, and evaluation. Description means taking a text and noting what you find there. It is an activity fostered by the 'close reading' of mid-century criticism, and greatly reinforced by the rise of literary stylistics in the last twenty years. Description is concerned above all with formal features, with lexis, with syntax, with figures of speech, with symmetries and parallels. It is the prerequisite for its partner, interpretation (which to be sensitively conducted needs detailed evidence), but also itself depends upon interpretation. That is to say that even the shortest text exhibits so many possible features for enumeration that you need some kind of interpretative intuition as a guide for what to look out for. Interpretation – which depends on the recognition that few communications can be reduced solely to their face value – constitutes the common ground between the disciplines on which this book rests. It has to do with working out and arguing for meanings, teasing out connotations, and listening for messages. Evaluation concerns the organisation of value hierarchies, judgments abut the worth of texts, and their standing in the eyes of teachers, publishers, and publics. Whatever our commitment to unconditional personal regard, we do constantly make value judgments – about humans as well as about books. For the purposes of this chapter, however, I suggest that we should withhold the desire to evaluate, thus freeing ourselves to notice all we can about texts.

There is one exception to what I have just said. This is because it is necessary to pay a little attention to what, for these purposes, counts as a literary text. 'Literature' in the sense I am using it here is plainly not a purely descriptive category; it has connotations of value. Readers have always discriminated between books, adjudging some to be important and enduring, others worthless, pernicious, or immoral. When the formal and institutional study of 'English' grew up in the early twentieth century it grew up fired with a sense of mission, a mission to preserve the best of the English heritage, and to promote a national language and culture which would reconcile social classes, promote spiritual health and nurture social harmony. In all its subsequent manifestations, and even as it oriented itself more and more towards the cultivation of the individual sensibility, the subject held on to the notion of a curriculum of great books. You might quarrel about where the boundaries came, who was included and who excluded, but the notion of literature as a canon of important books remained. Since around 1970 the discipline of 'Cultural Studies' has taken as its subject matter popular fiction, advertising, television serials, and the symbolic activities of everyday life. 'English' generally has not.

Now, there are a number of objections to the exclusiveness of the traditional approach, and its desire to rank books in hierarchies, mark down one author and promote another. The exercise is often socially snobbish in its attitude to popular fiction. It often works to exclude women, ethnic groups other than white, or others judged to stand outside the mainstream. However, I do want to be able to invoke some kind of criterion of quality to guide the choice of what to read. Some texts are more densely packed, offer more sustenance for the mind than others, even enable more interesting operations to take place upon them. In a word they are more demanding. Jackie Collins traps the mind, where George Eliot liberates. Criticism of Jackie Collins can and ought indeed to be written. One might speak of the debasement of women, the commodification of relationships, the fetichisation of parts of the body, and ask what, in Anglo-American culture such treatment of male–female relationships means. In the end, it is a matter of the reader's time. The cultural critic can perhaps justify the time spent analysing spy fiction, just as the cultural historian may be able to afford the time to read sixteenth-century sermons. The hard-pressed counsellor or social worker probably cannot.

What then of the qualities of those texts which we pick out for this kind of reading, and to which I am giving the loose label 'literature'? What kind of event is the close reading of such a text? What, to try again, can we use texts for? Many claims have been made over the years for the educative and humanising effects of attentive reading, and we need to see which of these speak to our present purposes. It used, for example, to be held that one of the things you went to great literature for was wisdom, that from your reading you could garner wise sayings, truths to add to your stock of knowledge about 'human nature'. While not wishing to disparage the pursuit of wisdom, I believe that the pursuit is far more arduous and uncertain than the Victorian connoisseurs of off-the-peg maxims would have allowed. Receiving lumps of wisdom would be a rather passive role, compared to the active participation in building symbolic structures which I am advocating. A concept which became prevalent among some artists and critics in the early twentieth century is perhaps more to our purpose. This took as its starting place the oddity of literary works (their formal devices, their pointed linguistic difference from everyday utterances) and spoke in terms of 'defamiliarisation', and 'estrangement'.

This is quite a simple notion to grasp and valuable for our purposes. In this theory, the oddity of art is actually the point. Just as a repeated stimulus soon ceases to affect us, so daily reality and our ways of talking about it become normal and unsurprising. We become anaesthetised, our perceptions dulled, there is much that we simply fail to 'see' in any lively sense. Politically and morally we do not ask questions, and get used to putting up with monstrous wrongs. Accordingly, the function of literary texts is to wake us up, to depict things in ways that are new and shocking. Maybe such an idea sets too high a value on literature, but the suggestion that immersion in some kinds of text gives a jolt to our familiar perceptual patterns is surely worth holding on to. It reminds us that seeing (in the broadest sense) is not the passive reception of outside stimuli, but the organisation of what we see into meaningful wholes. In the next chapter we shall have to speak about framing, and the patterns within which we notice our surroundings. Let us here note at least that one theory of why we should read offers us re-framing (viewing familiar things within alternative perspectives) as its core. There is, it seems to me, a helpful parallel with the therapeutic encounter: the boundaries and conditions of the sessions can have the effect of re-framing and defamiliarising what is said there.

Alongside this I would put my account of literary reading in terms of the cognitive work it calls upon us to do. Poems, novels, and so on draw our attention to aspects of human activity and experience which we might not otherwise have noticed, but then so too do works of history, psychology, or political theory. We learn from newspapers, magazines, and conversations with friends. How does 'literature' complement our other kinds of knowing? Part of my answer has to concern the way in which we are incited to perception. The very fictional nature of the text allows us to use it as what Jonathan Culler (1975) calls a 'model for intelligibility', an experiment in how meaning comes into being. This hypothetical element creates room for us to build up our own constructs.

Yet even this account of a laboratory of meaning-making is one-sided. For in naming and accounting for situations literature does not involve us at the cognitive level alone. To read a poem or a novel in the way I am suggesting is to enter into a dialogue between the cognitive and the affective and between concept and image. We become involved as persons, not as perceptual machines, an involvement akin to the practice of empathy in counselling. As we process a text we are engaged in an alternating rhythm of dissociation and reintegration which is scary and satisfying by turns. We have, so to speak, to put out fragments of ourselves, see them scatter as they attach to centrifugal objects, and yet find the patience and courage in ourselves to await their return.

Both reading and listening require us to move to and fro between different aspects of ourselves, and to test out the boundaries between the 'us' and the 'not us'. 'The sense of personal identity', notes Louise Rosenblatt (1978), 'comes largely from self-definiiton as against the "other", the external world of people and things. Literary texts provide us with a broadened "other" through which to define ourselves and our world' (p.145). Such self-reflexive motions of the mind characterise the kind of reading recommended here. Inasmuch as interpretation is our business, the text, while challenging us to make sense of it, will also frequently resist our attempts to reach final, unambiguous meanings. Literature is often valued precisely for this 'polysemy' as it is sometimes called, this capacity to convey several meanings simultaneously, to invite us into a process which cannot be finally closed.

It seems to be time to try to locate some of the things I have been saying here in a specific text. For this purpose I am taking a short poem, William Blake's 'The Clod and the Pebble' from his *Songs of Experience*, written in 1793.

THE CLOD & THE PEBBLE

'Love seeketh not Itself to please,
'Nor for itself hath any care,
'But for another gives its ease,
'And builds a Heaven in Hell's despair.'

So sang a little Clod of Clay
Trodden with the cattle's feet,
But a Pebble of the brook
Warbled out these metres meet:

'Love seeketh only Self to please,
'To bind another to its delight,
'Joys in another's loss of ease,
'And builds a Hell in Heaven's despite.'

What we shall do is recapitulate on the page the movements that a reader might make in trying to understand the poem, and then ask what we learn from this account of the sense-making process. On the face of it, the thing offers puzzles to the mind. We have a short poem, with a rather jingley metrical and rhyme scheme, reminiscent, in fact, of an eighteenth-century hymn. It consists of a dialogue between two rather improbable and distinctly low-status entities. It is arranged in a symmetrical form, the two outer verses formally paralleling each other more or less exactly while saying opposite things, and linked by a central stanza which identifies and sets off the speakers. The process of interpretation requires that we find a framework in which to account for the otherwise anomalous. At the same time it requires us to accept the risk of being infantilised. Hence, unless we are going to give up with the naturalistic exclamation 'pebbles don't talk!' (i.e. 'I'm not wasting my precious time on talking pebbles'), we need to find some way of accounting for this debate. Perhaps the poem belongs in an allegorical tradition where inanimate objects are allowed to express themselves, and take up moral positions. Perhaps as readers we need to get into parable mode. Then there is the substance of the dispute: the clod advances a traditional view of love – altruistic, able to overcome all things. The pebble is a cynic, portraying love as essentially egocentric, an imposition upon others of our own emotional demands. The two positions are baldly stated, and no narrative voice-over intercedes to explain or reconcile. Are we to assume that one of them has won the argument? The pebble speaks last, which is traditionally the place for the moral of the story to go. But our attempt to construct significances and make connections might lead us also to wonder whether the characterisation of the two speakers is indicative. We might prefer the clod's view of love, but we observe that the clod is shapeless, squidgey, and downtrodden. It takes the impression of whatever last happened to step on it. If we pursue this line of thought we get to thinking of the clod as a sentimental wimp, just waiting to be used as a doormat. On the other hand, pebbles are hard, can be used for breaking things, while being unbreakable themselves. Can we trust anything such a hard-baked creature says?

I see no way of reconciling these positions, or declaring finally what the poem is 'about' (apart from asserting that it portrays an unsettlable argument about the nature of love). I don't think anyone else can settle it for us either. But I note that in the search to get things straight, the reading mind moves outwards through progressive levels of contextualisation. The further move would be to locate the poem within the context either of eighteenth century theories about love, or of Blake's other work, noting along the way that our bare printed text is shorn of the engraving with which he illustrated his work. Perhaps the most helpful thing I can do here is to point to the dialogic nature of much of Blake's work, the way the *Songs of Experience* answer and enter into dialogue with the *Songs of Innocence*, the one taking up positions that are apt to seem naive, sentimental even, the other more reductive, jaundiced views. When he put the two sets of poems together, Blake called them *Songs of Innocence and of Experience* and added 'Shewing the Two Contrary States of the Human Soul'. This notion of contrary states, and of the self in dialogue runs through Blake's work. For that same reason it is risky to quote his sayings, quotation tending to hang the aura of truth upon wordings in process; having said 'Blake says' you are apt to find him saying the opposite somewhere else. Nevertheless, I find pertinent this statement from the (roughly contemporaneous) *Marriage of Heaven and Hell*:

> Without contraries is no true progression. Attraction and Repulsion, Reason and Energy, Love and Hate, are necessary to Human existence.

Such an utterance does seem to provide us with a context for the argument between the clod and the pebble, and suggest that perhaps what we are dealing with is not 'the truth' (according to Blake love is self-seeking...) but dialogue, voices disputing with each other like characters in a play.

From this rapid account of Blake's poem I want to extract a general point for my own argument. It has to do both with the nature of the literary text, and the nature of the relatedness of the reader to that text. Blake's little poem provides us with a working example of the idea of meaning held in suspension. The poem mimes the actions of the mind. In turn the reader's mind performs a sequence of actions of which none is necessarily final. There is rarely an exclusively correct meaning – ambiguity, so far from being a sign of inept writing, may be a positive value. Many literary texts work this way, provoking the making of meanings, but not necessarily foreclosing on what the results of that meaning-making may be. Furthermore, it suggests that strangeness – here the oddity of the participants – may be a feature of text that (in demanding explanation or re-framing) pushes us into taking the activity further than might at first have appeared necessary. These points and others may be developed by taking another short text from a different time and milieu.

'The Train from Rhodesia' was written by the contemporary South African novelist Nadine Gordimer. and published in 1953 (the text is in the appendix). Once you have read the story, we shall again try to enact ways in which as a reader you might work upon it. A first step might be to scan the story for whatever strikes you. For obvious reasons I cannot enact that process for you, but scanning a text without any fixed intention to emerge from it with results can be a very important stage in the reading process. Here we might notice things like a certain tendency to the anthropomorphic ('the flushed and perspiring west'), the fact that the characters are minimal and not even given names, the lack of traditional speech markers and even sometimes syntax ('The young man outside'). The story takes but a few minutes to read, and its 'real' time is short, perhaps half an hour at the most. There is no clearly marked narrative voice (the voice of the book) to guide us in what to think; in fact, the whole thing seems understated, perhaps a bit thin. Where do we go from there? Giving time and patience to pieces of language is an element of the activity for which I am arguing. We need to go from the impatient 'so what?' to the more delicate and attentive 'and so?'.

Let us begin with the notion of semantic field. If we attend to the vocabulary of any text we will generally find that lexical items can be grouped in families, that certain sets of items emerge as important. Broadly speaking, detail in a story can fulfil one of two functions. It can be used for purposes of verisimilitude, to construct a convincing picture of reality, or (as objects so often will in our own daily experience), it can take on further significance and start to become what we are apt to call 'symbolic'. We are looking out here for prominent signifiers, and noting that prominence may arise either from repetition (something that keeps coming up in a discourse is likely to be important) or from deviation – the item is handled in a way that deviates from the usual. Repetition alerts us to the recurrence of animals (live/dead; real/wooden) and of food – mutton, sponge-cake, meat cooked with onion, bread, an orange, and chocolates. The notion of deviation seems applicable to the train which both begins and ends the story. This train has animate, even human characteristics. Building on a not so unusual way of describing a train (we might refer to a train snaking along a winding track) it is described in reptilian terms (it 'cast the station like a skin'), but also as a 'resting beast'. More humanly it calls out, in an odd phrase, 'along the sky' 'I'm coming... I'm coming', but gets no answer. The novelist obviously thinks that the cry and the lack of answer are important, for the same motif is repeated at the end.

Let us hold on for a minute to the cry and the silent landscape, while noting the emergence of possible significances from the unanswerable. Another deviant thing about the train discourse is the arrival at the station: 'The engine flared out now, big, whisking a dwindling body behind it; the track flared out to let it in'.

Even if we accept that 'flared' may represent an attempt to render the perspectival effect of a moving object getting nearer, the track presents problems. We know that in fact railway lines stay the same distance apart. This train seems to be reptilian, snake like, phallic even. There may be a resonance, in a story about a young couple returning from their honeymoon, of the (male?) train penetrating the (female?) landscape ('I'm coming'). Let us hold on to this in our minds and come back to it.

What about the characters of the story? Here the reader has to build up a picture from minimal clues and implications. Two passengers in particular are brought to our attention, the young woman and her husband who bargain for the wooden lion. In the middle of the story and again at the end we are allowed access to the mind of the young woman (although not to that of the young man – we never know what he thinks), and a mind style is briefly created. The questions and the repeated sentences without main verbs ('But the wooden buck...' 'The young man outside') drop into place as a way of notating a 'stream of consciousness', suggesting the passage of unformed thoughts and feelings through the brain. It is from this too, and without narrative intervention, that we learn their situation: 'The young man outside. But he is not part of the unreality; he is for good now.' The episode over the purchase of the lion releases a bitterness in the woman against her husband (she is shocked that he has cheated the old man), and a deep feeling of disillusionment which, we gather, she has felt before. 'A weariness, a tastelessness, the discovery of a void made her hands slacken their grip, atrophy emptily, as if the hour was not worth their grasp. She was feeling like this again.' Note the way in which the bodily dimension of thought is captured, but also (in terms of our interpretation) the way in which the episode of the lion is used to focus things about the young woman and her marriage which are not stated but left to our imaginations to follow up. There is at least a suggestion that she has realised things about her husband which she had not understood before. A moment, an occasion, often has this symbolic force in the tales told in life as well as in books. An icon, a vivid but fleeting scene becomes the vehicle for a psychological percept, and the mnemonic to which the memory is attached.

That, however, with its implicit judgment that the story is 'about' the young couple, is to maroon our reading at the psychological level. I suggest that the story can simultaneously be read in another (call it sociological or even political) dimension. To pick up this thread it is necessary to note a binary structure to the story, characterised by the opposition inside the train/outside the train. The outside is a world of hot sand, bare feet, skeletal dogs, and dependence on the train to bring good things (money, food). The inside is a world of comfort, and plenty, where you can not only afford chocolates, but even to throw the ones 'that no one liked' (under the circumstances plainly ironic) to the dogs. The train exudes its own surplus in the form of the smell of cooking, which the dogs go to inhale. Implicitly we have a world of blacks and one of whites. The two worlds are clearly demarcated: 'Through the glass the beer drinkers looked out as though they could not see beyond it'; as the train gets ready to leave, the men who have got out to stretch their legs spring on 'clinging to the observation platforms, or perhaps merely standing on the iron step, holding the rail; but on the train, safe from the one dusty platform, the one tin house, the empty sand'. We do not need to import much contextual knowledge to suggest that the train, which has penetrated this land as the husband has penetrated the wife's body symbolises white southern Africa. On board is luxury (people returning from holiday), outside hardship. The inside and the outside are linked through a form of exchange in which the passengers bargain for the work of local craftsmen, wooden objects which thus become tourist knick-knacks ('How will they look at home? Where will you put them?'), and throw a few pennies or bits of food in for good measure. One aspect at least of the economy of the region (the waiting artists) is built round tourism.

The story, I suggest (and the same is true of most narratives), can be read on either a psychological or a sociological plane (about a relationship or about southern Africa). But the either/or formulation is not enough. Different meanings may be entertained simultaneously, although the effort to do so requires listener or reader to be willing to tolerate ambiguity. The two planes throw mutual light on each other. They may even be interlinked by a third.

To detect the presence of this additional layer we need to look at the artists. 'All up and down the length of the train in the dust the artists sprang, walking bent, like performing animals, the better to exhibit the fantasy held towards the faces on the train.' It is often the case that a work of art will contain within itself references to the making of works of art. They do not need to be the same art forms – a novel may foreground painting, a painting a musician. Here we have craftsmen who make wooden animals, who are themselves likened to animals, who perform for the benefit of the privileged on the train. The presence of the artists and their work, and the bargaining for pieces to take home raise in this story the question of its own value. What is art (including this story) worth and how is it valued? Who wants it? Is it for entertainment or enlightenment? Is the artist just a performing circus animal? The links which are formed lead us back to the young woman on the train. If there is the ghost of an identification between the novelist and the artist in wood, there is a further trace which connects the novelist with the young woman, confused and shamed by her husband's knock-down purchase of the beautiful lion. 'One-and-six. One-and-six. One-and-six for the wood and the carving and the sinews of the legs and the switch of the tail. The mouth open like that and the teeth. The black tongue, rolling, like a wave. The mane round the neck. To give one-and-six for that. The heat of shame mounted through her legs and body...' The somatic heat when it comes is not sexual but fired by shame. In this moment she discovers something about her relatedness to her husband certainly, but also about her relatedness to her society. We are not told what precisely she has discovered (another kind of narrative would have had the narrator step in to summarise and explain), but the story implies a series of connections that link black Africa, the old man ('the artist had delight in the lion'), the young woman, and the shadowy figure of the story's own artist, the (female) novelist on the verge of a lifelong campaign against apartheid.

The point of giving this account of Nadine Gordimer's story (apart from introducing you, perhaps, to her work) was to demonstrate with specific detail some of the more general points about the nature of literary study. I have been especially concerned to draw out the aspect of collaboration, of the dialogue between the text and the mind of the reader in the weaving of a web of significances. Is there a hitch? One of the arguments often directed against this sort of work runs like this: aren't you reading all this in? the author can't possibly have intended all that. After all (and with the best will in the world) people like me have a professional interest in propagating criticism and spawning literary argument. It is perhaps understandable if literature classes or individual readers sometimes react to teachers and critics with irritation or incredulity. But I hope that everything I said in the earlier stages of this chapter substantiates the claim that *all* reading is 'reading in'. Without the active collaboration of the reader, the text is only some marks on paper.

As for the author's intentions: perhaps she didn't intend all that in any conscious or planned way. But reflection on our own conversations should remind us how often we didn't realise until afterwards the full import of what we had said ('I could have bitten my tongue'), or how we found significances rising to the surface of what someone else was saying. We do not exercise total conscious control either over our own utterances or over the decoding powers of others. Private symbolisms pass into the public domain, where the originator can no longer control their significance. I would go a step further and claim that the wish to stop further unravelling of significance ('you're reading all this in') may actually represent a fear of unconscious process, a policing of the image by the sterile literalism of the ego. The 'denial of the demons', argues James Hillman (1983) in Jungian vein, 'leaves the psyche bereft of all persons but the ego, the controller who becomes super ego' (p.65).

Central to the thesis of this book (and this will not come as a surprise to those trained to listen to others or to work with groups) is the notion that human situations and the human mind are infinitely complex, that summings up or slogans – necessary though they may sometimes be – are rarely adequate to capture the subtlety of what happens or what humans are thinking and experiencing. The simplest remark (had we time to pursue it) is clouded with nuance and fine shades of meaning. We cannot possibly be tuned in to all these all the time, but we can educate ourselves to improve our receptive range. To read and listen sensitively we also have to be aware of what provokes and sets going our attention and curiosity. We have to struggle against our (natural) desire to simplify and normalise, against the routinising of perception and thought. We need to listen out for other voices and the stirrings of other energies. Let us return for a moment to 'The Train from Rhodesia'.

Frequently in fiction (and perhaps even more so in poetry) we come upon things for which we can give no satisfying explanation, items which defy our attempts to slot them neatly into place. One such example occurs in 'The Train from Rhodesia'. It is the man who walks from one end of the train to the other 'interrogating the wheels'. As I noted before, detail in a narrative may simply connote reality. On long journeys they used to check the wheels for cracks, and the man may just be an example of the sort of thing you would have seen if you looked idly out of the window of a stopped train. But then why does the story make quite such a point of him? He may be (though this is quite unsettlable) an instance of a mysterious figure who sometimes turns up in stories, a messenger, some one who has something to say to which the protagonists should attend. Again, he might be a reincarnation of the little peasant by the track in Anna Karenin's dream, in which case he refers to another train and another disastrous marriage. Either way, he calls out something which the passengers cannot hear, and the moment itself encapsulates all those things in the tale which we cannot quite hear, and about whose significance we might brood. Like the passengers, we are only travelling through this world, we do not fully understand it. Similarly, no one answered the train's cry at the beginning or the end of the story, and we are thus urged to some sense of a world of mutual incomprehension, or at least of the impossibility of dialogue between two sides. I am using the man by the track as my example of all those ways in which the smooth flow of our reading may snag on something odd about a text. It may be a discrepancy, a break in the tone, an inconsistency, an out-of-place feeling detail. Such occasions, when a text throws them up, often impede the forward thrust of our reading and compel us to re-align our sense of what is going on. When reading, as when listening, we want to push on towards meaning, to get things straight at once. Such an urge often leads us to snap decisions on how to understand what we hear.

Certain kinds of textual moment resist this treatment (twentieth-century poetry is notorious for resisting casual attempts to milk its meanings) and force the reader to make detours through unknown territory. Iconic objects (details realised with a deal of visual force) frequently act in this gritty way, their potential meanings hooked onto our memories by their visual appeal. The wooden lion itself is our example here. Although it is described in some detail, we do not know exactly what the lion signifies. Its purchase becomes, as we have noted, the focus for a disagreement between the husband and wife; at the end it lies abandoned on its side in the corner. Emotions and memories, we know, attach to objects, and the story even makes a point of this: 'She sat there not wanting to move or speak, or to look at anything, even; so that the mood should be associated with nothing, no object, word or sight that might recur and so recall the feeling again...' But the lion is irreducible: we cannot nail it once and for all by saying the lion equals male pride, or art, or Africa, or anything else. In this way a textual object may go on irritating the desire for significance. It is tempting to quote Blake again: 'The wisest of the Ancients consider'd what is not too Explicit as the fittest for Instruction, because it rouzes the faculties to act' (Letter 23 August 1799). And that which is sharply visual may also enable us to travel the circuits between iconic and conceptual parts of our minds.

We are tangling here with a subject that will run in and out of this book, the subject of symbolism. While we think of certain kinds of signifier as symbolic we also need to acknowledge their refusal to fit into any exact scale of equivalence. Wooden lions go on generating meanings in a way that is not accounted for by the rather thin conception of symbolism people often work with in the everyday ('It's a phallic symbol'). Its irreducibility accounts for some of that aura of significance which we sometimes think of symbols as possessing. There's nothing particularly mysterious (let alone mystic) here, but it does appear that some signifiers cause the mind to worry on in pursuit of significance without at the same time fixing achieved significance in formalin. The mind finds itself subject to the contradictory pressures of being simultaneously tempted to make meaning and repelled from its own results. In the final stage of this chapter we must attend to the relationships between different levels of meaning. To do this we must look briefly at the subject of fantasy.

Fantasy is another of those topics on which literary study, psychotherapy, and the study of groups meet. It is the domain of all those wishes and beliefs that the mind entertains which are not governed, or are only loosely governed by pragmatic considerations. A huge range of possibilities is included here. There is individual fantasy, ranging from consciously entertained daydream, the mental performance of acts or setting up of situations which we probably would not carry out in life, to unconscious beliefs which we only become aware of through slips and mistakes, or through the surprising responses of others. There are social fantasies – irrational beliefs widely held or encouraged within a culture (the animate and redeeming power of money). It seems likely that to all our thinking there is a penumbra of fantasy: shadowy parts of the mind in which we entertain beliefs, wishes, hopes, and apprehensions that our rational, daylight minds would reject. We both believe and do not believe in the malign intentions of objects, we slip into attributing omnipotence to our more assertive colleagues, we dread the end of the world in minor setbacks. All the signs are that on any given occasion we draw on vast tracts of ourselves – areas about which we know very little, but which may influence our behaviour in significant ways. If I accidently erase a computer file, the strength of my reaction (shock, muscular tension, nausea) indicates that symbolically, in fantasy, this loss 'stands for' worse losses, a hole in memory incommensurate with everyday fact. Counsellors and therapists are trained to listen out for the traces of the unacknowledged in acts and speech. Here is our parallel with literature. For here too we are dealing with manifest and latent, that which is apparent, as we say, 'on the surface' and that which lurks beneath or behind the words.

Fictions we may see as themselves fantasies. Not only do novels and the like contain within them much fantastic content, but fiction itself may plausibly be seen as a socially legitimated fantasy. When we enter into fictions, play over the occasions in our heads, imagine the scenes, identify with some characters and indulge hatred of others, we are engaging in something very akin to daydreaming, only in a form which is given public accreditation, available in the public world. We invest signifiers with unconscious energy. This is true even of realist novels where the governing fiction is that we are dealing with a real world, plausible scenes and characters. There are other kinds of fiction (ghost stories, futuristic fiction, or Angela Carter's novels) where the fantasy content is foregrounded and unavoidable, forcing us to re-take our bearings and re-set our boundaries. Engagement with literary text enables us to move to and fro between levels of signification and between levels of experience, re-thinking our deployment of significance as we go. This movement between levels and in and out of orders of significance can be seen as a form of play.

Fictions occupy a strange half-way status between the subjective and the objective. Composed of language, and dependent upon conventions which are in the public domain, they invite subjective participation on the basis of fantasy. One way of putting this is to suggest that immersion in a fictive world gives us access to parts of ourselves (and aspects of our enmeshment in our culture) which we do not normally want to know about or acknowledge. There is an analogy here with Freud's account of wit. The joke or the pun enables a temporary evasion of the censor, allowing the expression of an otherwise inhibited wish.

In the same way the text (which we can always assure ourselves is not after all real) allows the engagement of unrecognised parts of ourselves. Even if it were simply a matter of freeing up clogged expression, that might be valuable in itself. But once again, a topographical model of mind (say, here, the irruption of material like lava from suppressed layers) is not quite adequate to the case. For it may not simply be that all this material is standing by in a state of readiness. Clearly, it sometimes is: someone who explodes with rage about what appears to a third party to be a trivial incident presumably has ready (just beneath the surface, as it were) a scenario that calls for such a response (e.g. I've been thwarted all my life; the next time will be the last straw...). Individuals, like social groups, have their favourite stories to tell themselves. But it seems likely that the world of our hidden selves is not simply one where beliefs and scenarios exist all formed and ready to go, but a place of potencies and latencies, desires and fears which have not yet acquired shape. The generative response to textual cues may actually be the occasion on which such fears and desires first take form, first become embedded in a potentially tellable narrative. Hence, presumably, the enormous importance of identification with heroes and heroines or the ingestion of standard plots as structures within which potential selves can be enacted in safety. Romance or soap opera probably do an enormous amount to supply people with shaping fictions for their own lives.

In our relation to fiction some of the rules of everyday life apply and some do not. This is my reason for alluding to play: a bounded area within which it is possible to experiment with making patterns that extend the possibilities of the self and of action. Culture, as Winnicott (1971) has shown us, is in direct continuity with play, located in what he calls a 'potential space' between the individual and her environment. If the cultural sub-set literature is a laboratory for exploring the interface of self and society, then slow reading (of the kind I am advocating) is both a vehicle for experiencing that process more profoundly, and a means for observing the process in action by attaining some distance from it. In this kind of play, fantasy (which courts omnipotence) is brought up against a resistance imposed by the otherness of the public material. Thus cultural form may be distinguished sharply from daydreaming (which acknowledges no limitation). Our engagement with forms – fuelled as it is by pleasure and by unconscious energy – provides us with one way of re-defining and extending our being in the world.

SUGGESTIONS FOR FURTHER READING

Catherine Belsey (1980) *Critical Practice.* London: Methuen.

Ronald Carter (ed) (1982) *Language and Literature: an Introductory Reader in Stylistics.* London: Allen and Unwin.

Terry Eagleton (1983) *Literary Theory: an Introduction.* Oxford: Blackwell.

Barbara Hardy (1975) *Tellers and Listeners: the Narrative Imagination.* London: Athlone.

Wolfgang Iser (1978) *The Act of Reading: a Theory of Aesthetic Response.* Baltimore: Johns Hopkins UP.

Toril Moi (1985) *Sexual/Textual Politics.* London: Methuen.

Sue Roe (1987) *Women Reading Women's Writing.* Brighton: Harvester.

Raman Selden (1985) *A Reader's Guide to Contemporary Literary Theory.* Brighton: Harvester.

Raman Selden (1989) *Practising Theory and Reading Literature.* Hemel Hempstead: Harvester.

Susan Sellers (1991) *Feminist Criticism: Theory and Practice.* Hemel Hempstead: Harvester.

Jeremy Tambling (1988) *What is Literary Language?* Milton Keynes: Open UP.

Jane P. Tompkins (ed) (1980) *Reader Response Criticism.* Baltimore: Johns Hopkins University Press.

CHAPTER THREE

Interactive Reading I
Poetry

Our agenda at the end of the last chapter embraced a number of related issues. All of these concerned the nature of the activity that we undertook if we set about the kind of reading that I was proposing. In this and the following chapter I shall attempt to explore in detail what this participative reading means in relation to individual texts. The individual discussions are used to exemplify general points, but also to develop specific thoughts about the connections between the reading process and the listener's involvement in the symbolic world of the client.

For practical reasons, this chapter will draw its textual repertoire from poetry, and that of Chapter Six will be drawn from prose fiction. It is important to emphasise that this approach does not imply the existence of an absolute distinction between poetry and prose, just a way of coping with the problems of handling the textual material in a small compass. I hope that, taken together, the two chapters will prove to be complementary, and prompt insights that apply to the reading of any sort of literary text. The somewhat arbitrary division between the two chapters permits me to focus on different topics in each. In this chapter I shall concentrate on sound and sound patterns; the notion of difficulty and impeded reading; and the kinds of thinking that poetry instances. The two following chapters are concerned with metaphor and the role of metaphor in thought and language, and with narrative. Chapter Six is predominantly concerned with narrative and modes of telling.

I have signalled that this chapter concerns poetry. What do I mean by poetry? While I would want to reject any suggestion that there was a hard and fast definition, or that one could equate poetry with an indisputable essence, it would be disingenuous to pretend that the term was meaningless. Even if we cannot separate poetry and prose along a clear line of demarcation, the term clearly has some pragmatic force. What do I mean by 'poetry'? We need a working definition that will enable this chapter to be focused on a kind of subject matter and its resultant form of reading. There are several possible ways in. One way is via the eye. On the page, poetry deviates from typographical convention in being laid out differently from prose. Typically, a poem lies oddly on the page, with more space round the edges, and broken up into lines. Other typographical conventions are flouted – lines tend to begin with a capital letter, breaks are not where we expect them.

By starting with these apparently superficial matters we can in fact hook our notions about poetry onto the discussion of defamiliarisation in the previous chapter. For, clearly, one thing poetry foregrounds is deviation – deviation from the linguistic norms of everyday life, both spoken and written. Typographical deviation is one among a number of formal subversions of the expectable. The eye may be alarmed by the sight of a poem. We must, however, complement this account of visual difference by referring also to the ear. For the principal reason why poetry *looks* different on the page is because it *sounds* different: the visual is a score for the aural. Without dwelling on literary history, it is worth remarking that poetry has its origins in song, and song (think of pop lyrics) is the form of activity with which it has most in common. Poetry, we might say, is a way of transmitting meanings where the sound properties of the medium are fore-grounded. Through a whole range of devices (including the traditional resources of rhyme and regular metrical pattern) poetry alludes to the resources of the physical voice. It is also true that those forms which work with a pronounced phonological scheme are (quite literally) more memorable than prose. Once you have grasped the template – blank verse, ballad measure, or whatever – it is much easier to slot into it the necessary words which hold each other in place in the pattern. Even while it is broadly true that in recent history poetry has tended more and more to be devised for private reading (moving thus away from its roots in public recital), poems still require us to attend to a dimension of language which in the last chapter we were able virtually to ignore. A poem, even a poem shorn of traditional metrical or rhyme devices, and even if in fact you read it silently to yourself, typically poses questions about voicing. Sound and meaning are locked into interrelation.

One implication of what I have just been saying is that paradoxically (given the drab seriousness with which so many people regard their school experience of poetry) poetry, like music, is a form of communication which is based on pleasure. It seems to be generally true that given the right conditions and when not under pressure or distracted, humans find the use of language pleasurable. Talking is widely found to be a pleasurable activity, and many adults retain at least the residue of their childhood pleasure in making meaningful sounds. Playground rhymes, and the speed with which children latch on to the most tiresome jingle suggest that an even greater charge of pleasure is obtained from making meaningful sounds that also have a phonological pattern. The discovery of rhyme is a delight that wears off rather quickly on adults, although the success of phrases like 'loony left' and 'naughty but nice' bears witness to the continuing love of alliteration (front end rhyming) among English speakers. What I am suggesting is that poetry potentially puts us in touch with a childhood delight in language and its sounds. It is pre-eminently a playful way of using language, though this is serious play. One might speculate that it is precisely this regressive, even infantile quality that helps to account for the generally low esteem which poetry now enjoys in our culture. Poetry, it is widely felt, cannot be truly serious as compared to the language of the white paper, or committee minute. Meanwhile, play has been widely identified with frivolity, and is catered for elsewhere.

OCCASIONS FOR READING

The invitation to read a poem is an invitation to be present in the actual experience of reading. It asks us to attend to all the things which happen as we read in addition to operationalising extrinsic meanings. The activity of reading poetry thus stands at the opposite extreme from reading for purely instrumental purposes, a skill we have all learned, but which leads you (in Louise Rosenblatt's (1978) words) to 'push the richly fused cognitive-affective matrix into the fringes of consciousness' (p.40). So far, my working definition has worked from deviance, the oddity of poetry compared to 'ordinary' speech. I should add that one of the principal justifications put up for poetry in our own century is that it also differs from everyday utterance in being even more densely packed with meaning. Whether or not this is true of all poetry, it is an argument to which we shall return later. First I would like to explore the intertwining of pattern and meaning through a specific example.

As a starting place we could use a poem by a contemporary poet who has successfully swum against the twentieth-century stream in making much use of formal devices such as rhyme and metre. This is Tony Harrison's 'Fire-Eater'.

> My father speaking was like conjurors I'd seen
> pulling bright silk hankies, scarves, a flag
> up out of their innards, red, blue, green,
> so many colours it would make me gag.
>
> Dad's eldest brother had a shocking stammer.
> Dad punctuated sentence ends with but...
> Coarser stuff than silk they hauled up grammar
> knotted together deep down in their gut.
>
> Theirs are the acts I nerve myself to follow.
> I'm the clown sent in to clear the ring.
> Theirs are the tongues of fire I'm forced to swallow
> then bring back knotted, one continuous string
> igniting long-pent silences, and going back
> to Adam fumbling with Creation's names,
> and though my vocal cords get scorched and black
> there'll be a constant singing from the flames.

Try reading this to yourself, preferably out loud. If possible, do not worry too much about what it means, but try to get a sense of the movement of the words and the feeling of the whole thing as an utterance. Emphasise the rhymes if that helps. We are dealing with a kind of language that does not necessarily give up all its meaning at once. What sort of things do we notice? One of the first things I note is that the poem has a clearly marked form: to be technical, four stanzas (the last two are elided) with a repeated rhyme scheme a,b, a,b; c,d,c,d, etc. Underneath each line, underscoring, as it were, the way you read it is a stress pattern giving five heavy stresses (accentuation, or increased pressure on a syllable) in each line. The rhyme pattern creates an expectation that is then satisfied by the arrival of the rhyme word as it were just in time. Patterning of all kinds (and we shall visit many kinds of patterning in the course of this book) works by creating a pleasurable expectation of sameness, but also (as in the convention of rhyme) a tension between sameness and difference, the waiting expectantly for a word that sounds similar but is actually different. A poem like Harrison's proposes simultaneously equivalence at the level of form and difference at the level of meaning. One possible consequence is a tension set up not only in the ear's expectations, but in our whole reading set.

Many people associate rhymed poems either with archaism, or with verse for kids, perhaps of a jokey nature. Thus 'Fire-Eater' sets up a tension between what may appear to be its light-hearted linguistic romping, and what we come to intuit as its serious subject matter. This tension mirrors the tension within the poem (and so within its basic metaphor of performance) between clowning and having serious things to say. The poem's subject matter *is* so to speak its own praxis: how you can find a way to speak the things about your past, and about your parents that you need to be able to say?

I do not intend to give a detailed reading of this poem here. I have used it to raise issues about patterning, and as an example of 'serious play'. The seriousness of the poem is evident even without the extrinsic knowledge that much of Harrison's subject matter here as elsewhere concerns the relationship between his upbringing in working class Leeds and where he is now as a jet-setting poet and translator, and also that this poem itself belongs with a sequence which reflects on his parents and his feelings about his parents. Patterning in the sense of an expectation of repetition is evident at the semantic as well as the phonological level. The main lexical fields concern language (inarticulateness vs. the articulateness of the poet); performance (conjuror, circus); Biblical story (Creation and Pentecost); and fire. Threading these together is the reference ('tongues of fire') to the 'speaking in tongues' recorded of the disciples at Pentecost in the Acts of the Apostles. This has traditionally provided a metaphor for evangelism, and a search for the poem's meaning would need to traverse the speaker's sense that he is called to speak on behalf of the vanished and inarticulate generations that preceded him.

From this brief excursion into a poem I am knocking together the lesson that the integration of the levels of sound and meaning (phonology and semantics) in a poem requires us to read in a way that gives itself to the experience of the reading as an event. By giving ourselves to that experience, I am arguing, we are actually enabled not only to assimilate meanings but also to enter into the making of meaning as a dynamic process. The reading of the poem traverses the ground between fantasy, half-formed perception, and 'final' articulation. To borrow an analogy from mathematical education, a poem will often 'show the working', rather than leaping straight from problem to solution. The problem that faces us here is that reading and writing poetry is within our culture a deviant activity, even among those for whom possessing and reading books is a normal part of life. It has not always been so, and is not indeed so all over Europe. I am applauding a form of activity which in a crowded life may well seem pretty pointless (if you're working, work, if you're relaxing, relax…). Yet I suspect that behind the various formed and half-formed objections to poetry which one hears lurk other potent, but less audible objections, among which intolerance for unconscious process may well be one. The process of reading which I have sketched comes perhaps too close to the irrational, to the potentially chaotic realm of pre-thought, to be altogether comfortable.

It is necessary, then, to point out the similarities between attending to the formation of thought in a poem, and attending to the inner world of a client. The further thought that I wish tentatively to explore is that it may be precisely the pleasure in the process to which we have to open ourselves, and which is actually most threatening. It is important to insist that I am talking about the co-dynamic of pleasure and purpose − attention to the experience does not preclude attention to the meanings that have been focused. I am not advocating some version of the doctrine of art for art's sake, but indeed calling attention to the possibility that, while we cannot simply harvest achieved meanings from poetry, reading it may fulfil quite practical functions. The medium may be the message, but many messages are worth remembering, may indeed help us in shaping our own perceptions and in finding words for our own and others' emotions. Let us look at three short poems, chosen for their proximity to counselling concerns.

The first is 'To Speak', a short poem by the contemporary poet (born in 1923 in Britain, but now living in the USA) Denise Levertov.

> To speak of sorrow
> works upon it
>   moves it from its
> crouched pace barring
> the way to and from the soul's hall −
>
> out in the light it
> shows clear, whether

> shrunken or known as
> a giant wrath –
>   discrete
> at least, where before
> its great shadow joined
> the walls and roof and seemed
> to uphold the hall like a beam.

I think that the meaning of this poem is sufficiently obvious to any one whose roles include an element of counselling, and shall restrict myself to pointing out how Levertov makes use of the archaic imagery of crouching (monster?), hall, beam, roof to allude to the monstrous, brooding power of an emotion that cannot or has not yet entered into the interpersonal, shared world of speech.

Let me follow that from a different poet and a different era, a sonnet written by William Wordsworth (1770–1850) after the death of his three-year-old daughter Catherine, and at a time (1812) when he has been widely felt to have lost his touch, in becoming the pompous, increasingly reactionary sage.

> Surprised by joy – impatient as the Wind
> I turned to share the transport – Oh! with whom
> But Thee, deep buried in the silent tomb,
> That spot which no vicissitude can find?
> Love, faithful love, recalled thee to my mind –
> But how could I forget thee? Through what power,
> Even for the least division of an hour,
> Have I been so beguiled as to be blind
> To my most grievous loss! – That thought's return
> Was the worst pang that sorrow ever bore,
> Save one, one only, when I stood forlorn,
> Knowing my heart's best treasure was no more;
> That neither present time, nor years unborn
> Could to my sight that heavenly face restore.

Perhaps commentary on a poem like this seems an impertinence. At risk of that impertinence, I want to draw attention to the way in which the poem enacts a moment of being: his attention seized by something else, the speaker has momentarily forgotten that his child is actually dead. It is a moment that must have occurred to all those who have undergone bereavement or a serious loss – a straying back into 'normal' ways of thought, and then the hideous jolt from that familiar pattern back to the fresh recognition of what has gone. 'That thought's return/Was the worst pang that sorrow ever bore,/ Save one...' The poem has to find a way of negotiating the fact that its speaker has momentarily forgotten his bereavement, has allowed himself to be carried away by a moment of joy, and is thus left with the guilt of having allowed himself to forget. Not an uncommon movement of emotion: my point is that the medium of the poem allows that movement to be explored and a human situation to be named. The fact that the poem asks to be *voiced* (starting off briskly, and moving to the plodding line 'That spot which no vicissitude can find') puts the reader in the position of re-enacting in some small measure the thought process which results in the poem. That process is a movement from the scattered and scattering nature of emotion to a kind of provisional order.

My third example also concerns an emotion and its expression. It is by Stevie Smith (1902–71), perhaps most widely known for her 'Not waving but drowning' and through Hugh Whitemore's play *Stevie*.

ANGER'S FREEING POWER

I had a dream three walls stood up wherein a raven bird
Against the walls did beat himself and was not this absurd?

For sun and rain beat in that cell that had its fourth wall free
And daily blew the summer shower and the rain came presently

And all the pretty summer time and all the winter too
That foolish bird did beat himself till he was black and blue

Rouse up, rouse up, my raven bird, fly by the open wall
You make a prison of the place that is not one at all.

I took my raven by the hand, Oh come, I said, my Raven,
And I will take you by the hand and you shall fly to heaven.

But oh he sobbed and oh he sighed and in a fit he lay
Until two fellow ravens came and stood outside to say:

You wretched bird, conceited lump,
You well deserve to pine and thump.

See now a wonder, mark it well
My bird rears up in angry spell,

Oh do I then? he says, and careless flies
O'er flattened wall at once to heaven's skies.

And in my dream I watched him go
And I was glad, I loved him so,

Yet when I woke my eyes were wet
To think that Love had not freed my pet

Anger it was that won him hence
As only Anger taught him sense.

Often my tears fall in a shower
Because of Anger's freeing power.

This presents us with difficulties in terms of the discrepancy between its apparently juvenile (even naive) register and its subject matter, and also formally in terms of its working to a pattern which it relentlessly converts into jingle. It may be that (as with some of Blake's songs – Stevie Smith has, I think, a lot in common with Blake) our first inclination is to dismiss it as childish. Let us look at the obstacles to assimilation which the poem presents. There is, as already noted, the jingley scheme: a stanza like 'You wretched bird, conceited lump/ You well deserve to pine and thump' seems positively to defy our ability to take it seriously. Then there is the problem of realism. Talking ravens, like talking pebbles remind us of the crude anthropomorphism of some children's books. These are not even consistently ravens, since they are equipped with hands. To some degree, the poem seems to be trying to get round the difficulty by claiming to represent a dream, in which as we all know metamorphoses and transformations of all sorts are possible. In a dream you could have a house with three walls out of which a raven could not find its way.

But we are also presented with a thesis to do with anger. This uses the metaphor of imprisonment to investigate the possibility that some one could be 'trapped' by a mental and emotional construct. Because the raven *believes* in the existence of the fourth wall it cannot leave the place despite there being no physical obstacle. It is a matter of what Blake called 'mind forg'd manacles', restraints created by the mind. The raven is trapped within its own drama of sadism and self-contempt. It is incapable of responding to love or of valuing itself enough to escape its prison. Clearly, the poem does have resonances with the work of counselling. And yet there is a further twist. The loving attention which the speaker of the poem extends to the raven is not sufficient to help it to find the way out, obvious as the way out may be. Offered a guiding hand, the raven throws a wobbley. In the end, what does get him going is the goading of the two ravens outside – and the rest we know. The poem's parable has articulated in narrative form an argument about self-hypothesis and about the ways in which your self-hypothesis can be changed. It makes no claims about how common such situations might be, offers no evidence. Positively, by its recourse to imagery the poem delays any attempt to assent to or dissent from an abstract proposition. Inasmuch as the thesis 'rings a bell' with the reader it is as he or she internalises the subject matter of the poem and is willing to apply the thesis to situations he or she has met.

The purpose of this rapid trip around three poems has been to substantiate the claim that there was much in the corpus of poetry that could speak fairly directly to any one concerned with how humans think their experience. It is, however, necessary now to return to the main argument of this chapter, which concerns the way poetry works and its bearing on the reader's construction of their own emotions and thoughts. This takes us back to matters of language and discourse. I want to develop the notion that poetry is (or is potentially for those who know how to read it) a 'language of change' (Watzlawick 1978), that a poem is or may be a model for an activity consisting in the working through of unhandleable problems into handleable ones. Poetry, like speech, is a symbolic means of representing and transforming your environment, but without any suggestion that this proposition should be read as 'merely' symbolic. We can emerge from the reading of a poem with a good idea, a creative way of perceptualising experience, yet that translation into our own terms must not be confused with the fullness of the experience of reading the poem itself. It is time to try to tease out more about the nature of the activity.

ANALOGICAL THINKING

Let me start by picking up a few threads. Poetry draws its force from the pleasure of using patterned language; added to that is the aesthetic pleasure of seeing complexity held and ordered. A poem invites us to a kind of reading that is not oriented solely to practical results (though poems may well speak to our own everyday world), but permits the reader to dwell upon their own reading experience. It licences serious play. This experience is likely to traverse multiple levels, moving between unconscious fantasy, 'rational' goal-directed thought, emotion, and memory. Our next task is to consider two related areas: one is the nature of the thinking which poetry may induce. This thinking is connective in forming links between conventionally separated orders of experience, and analogical in the sense that as we read we 'try on' conceptual patterns analogous to those which pre-occupy us in the day to day. The second area draws on matter discussed in the previous chapter – the notion of impeded reading, and how the reading mind copes with obstacles. Examination of the former area should lead on into the second and thus onwards into the account of metaphor that forms the bridge to Chapter Six.

To enter into a poem is to enter into the generation of meaning. You as reader participate at a number of levels of organisation as you read a poem, and the presence of multiple ways of organising meaning opens up the possibility of yet more around what appears upon the page. You pass from one scheme – syntactical, logical, formal – to another, and the effect is to prevent repose upon a final meaning. At the same time you are given the working example of re-framing possibilities yourself, a stimulus to mental activity and pattern making arising from trying on likenesses. A poem will frequently offer (either overtly or implicitly) a hypothetical statement – such-and such a situation is like this; such-and-such a relationship is like that. This does not amount to a formal statement of an identity between the two, but rather (as in puns) a 'what if?' 'What if' we could equate a with b, what would it feel like? What consequences would follow for the rest of our perceptual arrangements? There may be no rational likeness between the items identified, but we might still engage in a 'what if?' The 'what if' might after all reveal what Jerome Bruner called an 'unsuspected kinship'. It would probably help to ground what I am saying through some brief commentary on another poem. Here is Ursula Fanthorpe's 'After Visiting Hours':

Like gulls they are still calling –
I'll come again Tuesday. Our Dad
Sends his love. They diminish, are gone.
Their world has received them,

As our world confirms us. Their debris
Is tidied into vases, lockers, minds.
We become pulses; mouthpieces
Of thermometers and bowels.

The trolley's rattle dispatches
The last lover. Now we can relax
Into illness, and reliably abstracted
Nurses will straighten our sheets,

Reorganize our symptoms. Outside,
Darkness descends like an eyelid.
It rains on our nearest and dearest
In car-parks, at bus-stops.

Now the bed-bound rehearse
Their repertoire of movements,
The dressing-gowned shuffle, clutching
Their glass bodies.

Now siren voices whisper
From headphones, and vagrant
Doctors appear, wreathed in stethoscopes
Like South Sea dancers.

All's well, all's quiet as the great
Ark noses her way into night,
Caulked, battened, blessed for her trip,
And behind, the gulls crying.

Here the primary 'what if' (or to phrase it more conventionally, the dominant metaphor) concerns the identification of a hospital with a ship (specifically an 'ark') putting out to sea. Arks have of course a specific set of meanings within western mythology, and a trace of this is present here. Within the poem's larger hypothesis (suppose for a moment we identified a hospital with a liner) are further subsidiary 'what ifs', above all the identification of the departing visitors with gulls calling, but also the references to 'siren voices' and 'South sea dancers'. If we look at a hospital in this light, making the sort of identification which it is quite possible to make in dreams, what other perceptions about being in hospital does it crystallise? One is the sense of the containedness of the world within and its clear separation from the world without: the voice of the poem clearly identifies with those on the inside ('Their world has received them,/As our world confirms us'; 'we can relax/ Into illness', a note that recalls the common perception that for the hospitalised the stress of visits is often quite hard to handle). As sometimes in the visual art of the twentieth century, a surreal image provides us with another 'what if' – what if the sick had glass bodies? – the image of 'rehearse... repertoire of movements... clutching/ Their glass bodies' may from one angle appear surreal. From another it catches the way in which those in pain, or who are newly deprived of accustomed mobility are likely to move: gingerly, as though their bodies were liable to break. The motion of the poem does several things at once, establishing the intensity of the inner world of the hospital as against the outer world of visitors, rain and bus stops; but also standing back to some degree from that world to see it as strange or even bizarre (the estrangement effect of 'vagrant/ Doctors... wreathed in stethoscopes'), and its denizens as dehumanized, reduced to assemblies of organs – 'We become pulses; mouthpieces/ Of thermometers and bowels'. Note how the half-concealed 'mouthpieces of... bowels' alludes to the public nature of excretion in hospital, with all the implied shaming dependence, a picture which consorts awkwardly with the reassurance at the end that 'All's well, all's quiet' – a statement which we may well decide to reshuffle as ironic.

I have taken this poem as an example so as to demonstrate a few of the ways in which a poem does not so much offer us formed statements (although of course some poems do) as draw us into the processes from which statements emerge. My next example is a much more stylised poem, a sonnet written in the very last years of the sixteenth century, Shakespeare's Sonnet 73.

> That time of year thou mayst in me behold,
> When yellow leaves, or none, or few do hang
> Upon those boughs which shake against the cold,
> Bare ruined choirs, where late the sweet birds sang.
> In me thou seest the twilight of such day,
> As after sunset fadeth in the west,
> Which by and by black night doth take away,
> Death's second self that seals up all in rest.
> In me thou seest the glowing of such fire
> That on the ashes of his youth doth lie,
> As the death-bed, whereon it must expire,
> Consumed with that which it was nourished by.
> This thou perceiv'st, which makes thy love more strong,
> To love that well, which thou must leave ere long.

Let us by-pass biographical speculation to observe that we have here a little drama in which a speaker laments to some one else that they are growing older. Implicitly, there are two persons present, the speaker and the addressee, both anonymous. Reading the poem involves the reader's mind in a tension between the security offered by the sonnet form (three syntactically and formally parallel quatrains, followed by a couplet) and the restless struggle to find words for growing older. It enacts what the critic Stephen Booth (1969) refers to as 'motions of the mind'. We have here, then, a small-scale drama in sense-making with affinities with the therapeutic session. A Shakespeare sonnet, he observes, typically invites the reading mind into an activity of shuffling and organising meanings. The reader 'is presented with a great many different ordering systems, none of which can reasonably be subordinated to any other' (p.117). Let us try to see how this is so.

The very first quatrain ('That time of year') starts by offering an analogy between growing older and the season of autumn, only to compress into this analogy the trees (metonymically related to autumn), but also ruined buildings, then returning to trees. Trying to grasp this, the mind moves back and forth among possibilities. 'I' embody a season, exemplified by autumn leaves on boughs (perhaps decay is just cyclical); they in turn remind the speaker of a ruined abbey – decay is irreversible – where, and the meaning now appears to refer simultaneously to boughs or to abbeys, 'sweet birds' (= choristers?) sang. The reader has just made some sort of sense of this, when we start again with another 'as if' – ageing is like evening, another cyclical suggestion, where we know that (at least as far as the individual is concerned) the process is irreversible. There are several routes through the quatrains. In turn, human mortality comes more and more into the foreground of each segment, until the fire and ashes of the third quatrain become transparently a way of talking about the death bed. Finally, the speaker turns to the observer who, having been simply the observer up till now, becomes the subject of the closing couplet, itself a rather glib signing off where a lesson is cleanly abstracted from what has gone before. The couplets of Shakespeare's sonnets often work like this, and perhaps, in putting forward something that would do as a conclusion (while not being adequate to the emotional range of the preceding poem) they mirror our desire to come out from complex statements with a formed solution, a moral, an 'it just goes to show.' To return to the poem as a whole: if, as Jerome Bruner remarks, poetry is 'a vehicle for searching out unsuspected kinship' (1982, p.36) this poem offers a sequence of analogical moves through which to speak of growing older and the approach of death. Yet there are two sides to this process: if poetic form and structure are modes of discovery, they are also and simultaneously forms for managing painful emotional content. They enable, let us say, both writers and readers to get a grip on material which might otherwise be too difficult to bring to articulation. The elaborate form and metaphorical sequence of Sonnet 73 *hold* the emotions generated by contemplating getting older and the imminence of death. The tension between repetition and difference is in some way deeply re-assuring. But it is not the re-assurance of covering your eyes. Much poetry offers us the possibility of attending to crucial emotional experiences – with our eyes open.

People have sometimes (and not altogether humorously) complained to me that poetry – especially modern poetry – is too serious, too cheerless and bleak. They often go on to make this a general complaint against literature. I'm not sure

I agree with the charge, but if there is something in it I wonder whether it has to do with the way that in a culture whose noisier manifestations are so given over to manic frivolity, poetry has gone on attempting to speak about things that we would in many ways rather not think about – passion, loss, the fear of failure, loneliness, and death. And such, indeed, are just the things that the lonely and those under intolerable stress may most need to talk about – and have to struggle to find a language in which to do so. Those who aim to help them could do worse than attend to the shifting struggle after meanings embedded in poetry.

THE USES OF DIFFICULTY

The previous section ended with a reflection upon the uses of form as a vehicle of discovery, and as a way of organising and managing difficult material. Form offers symmetry, but also repeatability: the essence of pattern is recurrence. Recurrence and expectability are re-assuring, and offer security even when, as Freud noted, the repeated pattern is in itself an uncomfortable one: which brings us to the radical ambiguity of form, for the existence of a template, a shape within which to say things, can be both liberating and constraining. Take the formulae of everyday life.

Social existence requires that we have a stock of easily said and understandable things to say, and such a stock certainly helps us to organise our experience into day to day shape. 'Great' we say when some one asks us how we found it; or 'it was interesting', or 'ygh, no *way*'. A very large part of our daily discourse is made up of formulae which offer rough approximations to what – had we had time to think longer – we might have wanted to say. 'God, it was awful.' 'She seems very nice.' 'Boring, dead boring.' We get by with these, and it is in any case true, as suggested in Chapter One, that language is in an important sense formulaic, that the notion of being able to mint language freshly all the time is a chimera. On the other hand, we are all aware at times of mismatch between the experience and the words; we speak of cliches and of stereotypes, both words for formulations felt to be inadequate to the reality or the particularity of what they purport to describe. Speech can easily become the gumming together of pre-fabricated phrases which fail to represent the specificity of things. Yet in the struggle to come to terms with new situations or break out of old ones, people often come up with statements of great force and power. There is an analogy here with the work of poems: they too struggle with difficulty to forge a new saying, a new way of talking. The emphasis of this section falls upon the concept of difficulty. Here I hope to pursue further that notion of impeded reading that was mooted in Chapter Two. There I suggested that in certain kinds of text the forward movement of our reading might be hampered by items that did not lend themselves to rapid assimilation. The suggestion was that such obstruction *could* – far from being merely a symptom of an incompetent or wilfully obscure author – serve a positive function in forcing our minds to deviate from the usual track into mysterious territory. Or to put it another way, a difficult poem may come in below the radar of defended rationality. Let us explore this a little further.

Obviously, difficulty in a text (as in any discourse) may simply arise from the author or speaker's incompetence, a technical failure in the use of the language. Such-and-such an article, we say, is 'badly written'; 'Dot has difficulty expressing herself'. On such occasions, difficulty takes on a random quality: the reader or listener bumps up against whatever she or he happens to bump up against. Here, I would prefer us to work with the hypothesis that difficulty is motivated, that certain kinds of utterances, certain kinds of texts are difficult not because of technical incompetence on the part of speaker or writer, but because the subject matter is itself difficult. It may indeed be at times a salutary discipline to try to put things in the simplest possible words, yet anyone who dogmatically asserts that 'it's really very simple' should be treated with the gravest suspicion. It is likely that the complexities they wish to suppress are those that are most injurious to their own case. Let us dwell on the hypothesis that the difficulties encountered in a poem or in the words of some one struggling to articulate a shocking experience are difficulties generated by the relationship between speaker and subject matter.

In a poem, such difficulties may be difficulties of lexis, syntax, cohesion, or a combination of all three. They may also be difficulties of pragmatics: who is the speaker, who the addressee of this utterance? Very often we will have trouble with attempts to integrate the elements we do understand within a larger scheme. That is to say that our drive towards meaning (I've got it, what she's saying is...), our desire to crack the code, is diverted. We can understand the thing in fragments, but we can't get the fragments to fit together. Obviously, one response here is irritation. Why can't she just say what she means and get on with it? We are tempted to put the book down in exasperation. I suggest this result may arise from too easy an acceptance of the omnipotence fantasy that 'it's all very simple', the delusion that there is a minimal gap between signifier and signified, that well-chosen words lead us straight (with no messing about) to things. Let's persevere. We see a portion of text; we expect it to yield up its meaning. It doesn't, and instead our reading skill is diverted, thrown off track by gaps, bizarre metaphors, opaque images, and unexpected transitions. This is disconcerting: we don't like to be defeated, and the unexpected and mysterious may lead us to thinking thoughts we did not intend to think. Instead of representing order, the poem suddenly seems to represent chaos. Small wonder if our inclination is to abandon it. There are, we may feel, enough chaotic and threatening situations in life without going out of our way to encounter them in our reading as well. My case is that the (admittedly small scale) experience of symbolic disorder bounded and framed within the poem gives us the opportunity to try out the potential as well as the limitations of our sense-making capacities. The form and bounded shape of the poem give us a framework within which to practise finding our way.

We can track back and forth across it, making an archipelago of sense. Perhaps if we return often enough the islands will join up. If not, we may still obtain glimpses of strange and wonderful creatures in the sea.

Not all poems, of course, are difficult in the sense I am suggesting. Enough, however, of the corpus of poetry comes within this category for it to be sensed as a forbidding mass by the late-twentieth-century lay person. Let me try to pin this sense of working with difficulty to some specific poems. The American poet Emily Dickinson may well be seen as a precursor of much twentieth-century poetry. Like so many nineteenth-century women writers she found ways of putting her isolation and lack of access to the public arena to use in conducting a scrupulous examination of the inner world.

> One need not be a Chamber – to be Haunted –
> One need not be a House –
> The Brain has Corridors – surpassing
> Material Place –
>
> Far safer, of a Midnight Meeting
> External Ghost
> Than its interior Confronting –
> That Cooler Host.
>
> Far safer, through an Abbey gallop,
> The Stones a 'chase –
> Than Unarmed, one's a'self encounter –
> In lonesome Place –
>
> Ourself behind ourself, concealed –
> Should startle most –
> Assassin hid in our Apartment
> Be Horror's least.
>
> The Body – borrows a Revolver –
> He bolts the Door –
> O'er looking a superior spectre –
> Or More –

Obvious difficulties include Dickinson's punctuation (the use of dashes as a scoring device), her idiosyncratic use of capitals, and the somewhat elliptical syntax. If we resolve to press on, the outlines of meaning start to become clear. There is clearly a binary opposition between the inner and the outer in which the inner is prioritised – 'The Brain has corridors – surpassing/ Material Place'. Equally, Dickinson is using Gothicry (deserted abbeys, ghosts) to characterise her outer world, only to turn round and say that the 'superior spectres' are actually within. Once the general drift of meaning has been established, statements that at first look odd ('Ourself behind ourself, concealed – / Should startle most') can be returned to, and fitted into the pattern of meaning. Yet this making of meaning, the trying out of possible paraphrases must always circle back to the specificity of the poem itself. Is the revolver of the final stanza a protection against burglars (equivalent to the intruder alarm and the rottweiler) or an instrument of suicide? The logic of the poem suggests the latter, but there's nothing to prove it: the suggestion is just there in the air, just as the final dash resists closure by leaving the end tantalisingly open, as though more and more statements to the same effect (or even worse) could go on being added. I have used Emily Dickinson's poem as an example of reading overcoming local difficulty. My final example involves a greater range of allusiveness.

D.H. Lawrence's 'Bavarian Gentians' presents multiple resistances to the mind of the reader.

> Not every man has gentians in his house
> in soft September, at slow, sad Michaelmas.
> Bavarian gentians, big and dark, only dark
> darkening the day-time, torch-like with the smoking blueness of
> > Pluto's gloom,
> ribbed and torch-like, with their blaze of darkness spread blue
> down flattening into points, flattened under the sweep of white day
> torch-flower of the blue-smoking darkness, Pluto's dark-blue daze,
> black lamps from the halls of Dis, burning dark blue,
> giving off darkness, blue darkness, as Demeter's pale lamps give off
> > light,
> lead me then, lead the way.
>
> Reach me a gentian, give me a torch!
> let me guide myself with the blue, forked torch of this flower
> down the darker and darker stairs, where blue is darkened on blueness
> even where Persephone goes, just now, from the frosted September
> to the sightless realm where darkness is awake upon the dark
> and Persephone herself is but a voice
> or a darkness invisible enfolded in the deeper dark
> of the arms Plutonic, and pierced with the passion of dense gloom,
> among the splendour of torches of darkness, shedding darkness on the
> > lost bride and her groom.

Some difficulties arise from the poem's allusive range, some from its syntactic structure. A first step should in any case be to try to read the poem through, feeling one's way, allowing vague meanings to shape in the mind. If you do that, the sound structure should start to become apparent. Thus, while this poem is technically in 'free verse' and so lacking the formal shaping given by clear metrical or rhyme patterns, we do have sound patterns arising from the repetition of sounds, phonemes (e.g. 's' in the second line) or whole words (e.g. the variations on 'blue' and 'blueness'). 'Darkness' repeated has a structural effect, partly in supplying the hint of familiarity (like a repeated tune – we hear the echo of 'dark' across the poem) but also paradoxically in the alienation effect created by frequent repetition. (A word repeated again and again starts to seem strange – try repeating a familiar word over to yourself: the semantic coating peels away, leaving you with a bare sound.) Thus repeated words both bind the poem together and simultaneously estrange with their incantatory quality, defying the usual rule against redundancy (i.e. don't use the same word repeatedly in close proximity). So we have the simultaneously semantic and phonic effect created by the repetitions of 'dark' and 'blue'. Another set of obstacles to instant reading is presented by the poem's use of Greek mythology, here the story of Persephone. (Persephone was carried off while gathering flowers by Dis/Pluto, the god of the underworld. Her mother Demeter/Ceres went to try to beg for her back from the god who had married her, and came to an arrangement by which Persephone would spent half the year in the upper world, half with her husband in the lower. Nineteenth-century scholars were inclined to see this as a redaction of an early fertility myth, an interpretation which Lawrence apparently shares.) The myth is re-enacted in the poem as the speaking voice seeks to follow Persephone into the darkness.

Syntax, too, obstructs easy reading, a problem located in the long sentences which form the two main sections. Yet it is perhaps from this structural difficulty that we may return to the question of meaning-making going on in the poem. In the first section the problem is that the syntax appears not to be going anywhere. We are held up waiting for a main verb. Having been offered a subject ('Bavarian gentians') we then wait while that subject is repeatedly qualified until we discover that our main verb is not even the transactive we might have expected, but an imperative addressed (presumably) to the gentians: 'lead me then, lead the way'. Although the structure of the second section is different (our main verb phrase appears early on – 'let me guide myself... down the darker and darker stairs') it too enacts impeded forward motion, stepping us slowly through a sequence of modifiers cumulatively linked – 'where... even where... and... or... and...' The whole poem seems to represent a meditation on the flowers, but also a verbal enactment of the journey it imagines, form and content mirroring each other.

My analysis so far, and its place in my argument suggests that difficulty and the reader's attempt to overcome difficulty is the central feature of reading poetry. This is clearly one-sided, and equally clearly does not apply to all poems. There is enough in it, though, to put before us the possibility that poetry offers us an opportunity to confront the strangeness of utterance, the otherness behind the words. Poetry can leave us feeling that even the most apparently commonplace statement may resonate in ways that discursive paraphrase fails to catch. Lawrence's poem speaks enigma, and even what appears to be a deliberate attempt to subvert everyday meaning.

We have already noticed how the repetition of 'blue' and 'dark' creates both internal cohesion and relational strangeness. But the two words also point us into what appears to be the semantic core of the poem, a lexical field organised around the binary opposition light/dark. What happens as the poem proceeds is that we are offered the contradiction dark = a form of light ('black lamps', 'giving off darkness', 'splendour of torches of darkness'). This affront to commonsense pushes us to reach out towards possible meanings. For example, that darkness is being offered us as a positive value, the entry into darkness (death?) a species of sexual initiation ('pierced with the passion of dense gloom'); the male poet identifying with the female goddess. Since in the parallel metaphorical scheme (surface/underground) depth is equated with darkness, we are offered the implied assertion that a journey into the depths is also to be positively valued. A shadowy pattern of inversion shows up as we consider. While the potential meanings of the poem are certainly not exhausted by these rather sketchy observations, the reader may gather some sense of the power of the poem to generate significance, above all to suggest possibilities with which the mind can experiment. At the end of the day, the darkness = light equation and the impeded forward motion of the poem are unassimilable, perpetually teasing the mind, inviting us to speculate upon the potential meanings of darkness and of going down into the ground, rather than to come up with straightforward equivalents.

The underlying argument of this chapter has been that poems offer us instances of meaning in process, occasions where the charge of pleasure derived from verbal form, or from overcoming difficulties, detains us to play with the formation of significance. Poetry provides both intellectual sustenance and practice for those whose business is communication and dialogue, a standing reminder of the interplay of all that is and all that is not said, the complicated play of statement and inference. In Chapter Six we shall turn to prose fiction. But first we will step back to look closer at a subject that has moved in and out of our discussion so far, the subject of metaphor.

SUGGESTIONS FOR FURTHER READING

George Lakoff and Mark Turner (1989) *More than Cool Reason: A Field Guide to Poetic Metaphor*. Chicago: Chicago UP.
Philip Davies Roberts (1991) *How Poetry Works*. Harmondsworth: Penguin.

Perhaps the best I can offer in the way of further reading is to suggest to you that you explore what this chapter has said in relation to some more poems. Anthologies containing examples of the work of more than one author are probably your best bet, enabling you to get a sense of which poets you yourself would like to find out more about. Some suggestions will be found in Part Two.

CHAPTER FOUR

On Metaphor

The word 'metaphor' has cropped up repeatedly in this book. It is time to explore further the concept of metaphor in its bearing upon both the 'art of listening' and upon literary texts. For the metaphor – of long-standing concern to the study of rhetoric and of literature – is now an object of attention in the domain of therapy as well. References to the work of Cox and Theilgaard and of Siegelbaum will be found in the suggestions for further reading at the end of this Chapter. Familiar to us, and the subject of much of the first chapter of this book, is the notion that language provides what Kenneth Burke calls 'terministic screens' through which human experience of the world is organised into sense. Metaphor is a central example of such screening, and the ideas so formed are apt to appear natural, simply 'how things are'. The point of picking out the subject of metaphor and holding it up to scrutiny is to exert a kind of alienation effect upon something that is usually so taken for granted that we are not aware of its organising power.

A dictionary definition of 'metaphor' is 'the figure of speech in which a name or descriptive term is transferred to some object to which it is not properly applicable; an instance of this' (*Shorter Oxford English Dictionary*). Because it is associated with the referential aspect of language, metaphor is often misunderstood as simply rhetorical clothing, a way of putting things to make them understandable, but unconnected with the real nature of the thing described. An example of a metaphor which does perhaps fit this description is given us by the teacher who uses the analogy of fluid in an attempt to make electricity comprehensible to an audience. The physicist knows that electricity is not 'really' like water, but the analogies of flow, pressure, and so forth, are useful explanatory devices. By this stage, readers of this book will have become used to the claim that the communicative system and the subject matter cannot be so easily separated: we cannot think subjects outside the language used to convey them. Our metaphors shape the way we think; they are not confined to the dressing up of truth, but reach deep into our conceptions of things.

A metaphor refers to one set of things in terms conventionally used for another. If I say that my office is a sea of paper, or that I have just done a mountain of ironing, I am transferring seaness and mountainness from their ordinarily accepted meanings. Detailed visualisation is not necessarily involved: no one is likely to think of the ironing as towering up against the sky, as exhibiting rock faces or patches of snow. It has more to do with the relationship between speaker and subject matter: what I express through these terms is that my attitude to the paperwork or the ironing contains within it the elements of feeling hopelessly daunted or wearily triumphant appropriate to the experience of seas and mountains. The dual theme of this section is, first, that the communal stock of metaphor helps to shape what is thinkable in a given culture; but second that, within the communal structures, individual speakers and writers exercise a degree of choice in the metaphors they use, so that metaphors are both indicative of thought habits and also (as Cox and Theilgaard argue) a locus of possible change. We need not be lived by our metaphors, any more than we need be totally scripted by our language.

In this section as elsewhere I have made much use of George Lakoff and Mark Johnson's wonderful book *Metaphors We Live By*. Their thesis is that language and thinking is very largely metaphorical, and that a large proportion of the metaphors we use is systemic. That is to say that they are organised in families (to put it metaphorically) which give rise to related metaphorical expressions. Some of these appear (even beyond the bounds of a single culture) to be fundamental ways of organising thought. Thus orientational metaphors such as up/down, where 'up' is usually thought of as desirable, 'down' undesirable, seem to be pervasive at least in European cultures – social class, status, health, mood, musical pitch, success and failure and so on, all appear to be thought on an up/down model. Again, darkness and light (presumably through association with being able to see your way) give rise to metaphorical sets for thinking about intelligence and understanding (a 'very bright/dim girl'; 'I'm in the dark about this'; 'I think light's dawned'; or words such as 'obscurity' or 'lucidity'...). An example of a less fundamental metaphorical family would be the set which equates energy with a fluid ('I feel wrung out'/ 'drained'; 'she's overflowing with energy').

The systemic nature of metaphor, once noticed, appears to be pervasive. Individual occurrences can be linked to the structure upon which they depend. For example, just now I spoke of trying to get a grasp of the nature of metaphor (incidentally, I did not of course *speak*: it is a fact of some consequence for how we think about writing that it is so often treated metaphorically as speech). Grasping an idea is based on two underlying metaphors, one that ideas are tangible objects, the other that mental operations are physical and tactile. Thus it is possible to 'get a grip' on monetary theory, 'grasp' the fundamentals of French grammar, 'put your finger' on the weak place in an argument, 'hold' a number of things in your head at once, 'get your mind round' a problem, and so on. Having your hands full, or being empty-handed speak for a condition and a stance. Metaphors often seem to involve translating phenomena that are abstract into terms that are more basic or sensuous in their application. Thus emotional or psychological properties are often put in terms of physical experience in the hot/cold continuum – a warm welcome, a frosty reception, a heated argument, a warm personality, and so on. Concepts are often treated as being solid entities with lives of their own independent of human minds – 'metaphors shape our thinking'; 'a psycho-dynamic orientation indicates...'; 'Group norms exercise considerable power over us'. In turn, the ordinariness and repetition of daily metaphorical usage shapes our understanding so that we think of (shall we say) feminism, monetarism, or quantum theory as having a real, autonomous existence outside human minds and purposes.

Now there is no doubt that metaphors often become invisible in the sense that they are so familiar that their source meanings no longer register with us (the lecturer who spoke of hammering out a perspective was clearly out of touch with the origins of the metaphors concerned). Inanimate things are commonly thought of as animate: this is so automatic that we rarely question the cognitive model implied in saying 'sod the stupid thing' about a car, or 'the sun's trying to come out'. The persistence of metaphorical systems points to their structuring power, the way in which metaphors provide equipment for thought. My argument is that raising metaphors to consciousness gives us evidence of how both cultures and individual human beings think; but also that (while some metaphors may be primordial, and beyond the reach of conscious choice) our metaphorical reper-toire may be changed. Poetry and conversation are both places where old metaphors may be re-vitalised, or extended, and new metaphors minted. Let us attend a little more to the question of how metaphors work; the effectiveness of metaphorical discourse in persuading speakers and listeners that the world is 'like that'.

Central to this conception of how metaphor works is that metaphors fore-ground some aspects of phenomena at the expense of others. Aspects which do not fit with the metaphor employed will be concealed. Take Lakoff and Johnson's example of 'argument = battle'. They point out that argument is typically thought of as a battle where one wins or loses, shoots down an adversary's case, attacks weak points, beats tactical retreats, and so forth. One can see that such an adversarial notion of argument has its roots (!) deep in the culture (think of law courts, or the tradition of parliamentary debate), but is simultaneously reinforced by the ways argument is talked about. The metaphor structures not only the way argument is thought about, but the very way in which arguments are performed. Such metaphors foreground or play up some aspects of argument (aggression, symbolic violence, the sadistic destruction of opponents), and conceals or discounts others. For example, that argument can involve an element of co-op-eration, where two or more parties give their time to an attempt to reach truth; that argument often involves heavily ritualised elements; or that 'winning' an argument is not necessarily purely a case of the triumph of reason. Or again (cf.

Chapter One) the conduit metaphor for language (ideas are things which pass through a conduit from one head to another) advances one aspect of language but masks others – the inadequacy of regarding an idea as an entity, or the performative aspects of language. The metaphor of 'centre', now so widely adopted in organisational parlance, promotes the idea of the hub of a system as being the place to be, and devalues other places in the system which correspondingly come to seem peripheral. And the current jargon of 'owning' emotions or projects – although apparently desirable – seems to represent an impress of the Thatcherite era upon our thinking. Obviously, examples could be multiplied.

If metaphor foregrounds and conceals in this way, then we need to learn to be aware of the influence of metaphor over our comprehension, not in the delusive positivist hope of attaining a metaphor-free world, but so as to stretch the meanings of our metaphors or develop new ones. Metaphors are among the moulds of our thought (may even be the primary moulds) and we need to have an eye to their limitations as well as their possibilities.

Yet there is a further reason why skilled listeners should be prepared to attend to the metaphors people use. It is likely that some metaphors are so basic as to be almost inescapable. With others, speakers exert considerable choice as to how they use them or even whether they use them at all. Like style, much about the choice of metaphor is personal to the speaker, and thus may act as a guide to the mind-style, the emotional and intellectual state and habits of the person using it. If someone says 'I'm banging my head on a brick wall', or 'I got torn to pieces', we recognise the conventional element (the culture makes the phrase available), but might also hypothesise that the speaker does actually find the phrase consonant with their experience. In other words, the possibility is always present that even what may appear to be conventional and unthought-about formulations and phrases do actually have some sort of purchase in the unconscious mind. Containing, as they do, an iconic (that is to say pictorial or sensuous) as well as a conceptual component, the images metaphors embody may originate in layers of thought that are usually inaccessible to inspection. Metaphor, suggests Siegelbaum, proceeds from primary process thought, and can act as a guide to the levels of thinking from which it proceeds. Someone who says 'I feel trapped' or 'It's all landed on my shoulders' is giving hints of powerful fantasies which may be built in to their whole bodily set towards certain places or occasions. Figurative language springs from strong affect. Psychoanalysts following Jacques Lacan would even go as far as to assert that symptoms themselves are metaphors in which the body or actions are used as signifiers. In this account, part of the work of psychotherapy is to translate symptoms back into linguistic forms where their power may be defused.

Since to be understood at all a metaphor must resonate with the listener, metaphorical attunement may open up the possibility of change. Metaphor, like other aspects of language, belongs in the forum of interpersonal negotiation, and

Siegelbaum (1990) – like Cox and Theilgaard – suggests that the attunement for which the therapist strives rests upon communication from unconscious to unconscious. She speaks of 'oscillation':

> Perhaps the most useful thing the therapist models for the patient is this psychological suppleness: the ability to shift attention and levels of consciousness, to range up and down, in and out, back and forth. This flexibility may be communicated at totally subliminal levels. (p.158)

Thus 'I feel as though I'm in a trap' is likely to resonate with both parties. Reflection might lead on to visualising the nature of the trap, who has set it, and questioning whether an enclosed space could not also be a secure place to be, somewhere to wait while regathering strength. Someone who visualises their working life as a battleground might be incited to vary the metaphor. What would happen if you substituted the metaphor of theatre for that of battle? Or again, body imagery such as 'I've lost heart', or 'that's hard to swallow' could be explored and perhaps made less gripping by working on where in the body particular feelings had their location and effect. In tending to dissolve the boundaries between categories, metaphorical acts continually incite us to what Cox and Theilgaard (1987) call *poeisis* (the act of making). Metaphor, as they put it in their learned and richly exemplified book *Mutative Metaphors in Psychotherapy*, 'exerts its mutative effect by energising alternative perspectival aspects of experience' (p.99).

So metaphors – like any other kind of language – are not inert, not unambiguous descriptions of 'real' conditions that lie outside their own domain. They occur in lived contexts, and provide us with access to thought in the making. At this point, the thesis being put forward in this section converges with one argument of this book as a whole. This is that those whose vocations and professional lives lead them towards focused listening can benefit from attuning themselves to symbolism (and its sub-set, metaphor) activated in poetry, novels, and plays. As Lakoff and Johnson (1980) say:

> A large part of self-understanding is the search for appropriate personal metaphors that make sense of our lives. Self-understanding requires unending negotiation and renegotiation of the meaning of your experiences to yourself. In therapy... much of self-understanding involves consciously recognizing previously unconscious metaphors and how we live by them. It involves the constant construction of new coherences in your life, coherences that give new meaning to old experiences. The process of self-understanding is the continual development of new life stories for yourself. (p.233)

Attentively to experience a work of literature is to be immersed in a discourse where symbolism is made and remade as you go along, where new metaphors cross the horizon of possibility, old ones acquire new meanings, and the generation of metaphor (and our dependence upon it) is illuminated. Reading is, among other things, time spent in the ambience of metaphor, and metaphor which ceases to be habitual and automatic and thus loses some of its power over us. It is also an experimental occasion for the production of symbolism. Meaning, I have claimed over and over again, is created in inter-personal space. It is no more just present in the words of the speaker or writer than it is just present in the mind of the listener/reader. Reproducing, or fabricating metaphors from new, represents a version of this process in action. Textual work both heightens our sense of metaphor, and stimulates us to the invention of new metaphors which extend our day-to-day understanding. In the last chapter, we spent some time with Shakespeare's Sonnet 73. There we were presented with a sequence of metaphors for ageing: 'That time of year thou mays't in me behold... In me thou seest the twilight of such day... In me thou seest the glowing of such fire...' That there are even more metaphors composited into this poem than is at first apparent is demonstrated by Lakoff and Turner (1989, Chapters One and Two, e.g., p.70). The point is not that the poet is working towards the ideal metaphor, an ultimate encapsulaton of all it means to be aware of growing older, and aware of others aware that you are growing older, but in the interplay of the different metaphors, all drawing on vivid iconic matter, but all partial, and all comple-mented by each other. To read the poem may be simultaneously to be moved by the half-humorous, half-rueful way it tries to capture a state of being, but also to be alerted to the trap concealed in assumptions of the naturalness or inevitability of particular metaphorical formulations.

I am suggesting that any particular discourse – any stream of utterance directed to another – will be found, on reflection, to be rich in metaphor. It would be useful at this point to take an example of the life of metaphor at work in such a stream, here chosen from a novel about growing up.

> The dirt path going down to the wooden footbridge is dry, dusty; the leaves of the trees which hang over it are dull green and worn out from the summer. Along the edge of the path is a thicket of weeds: goldenrod, ragweed, asters, burdocks, deadly nightshade, its berries red as valentine candies. Cordelia says that if you want to poison someone this would be a good way. The nightshade smells of earth, damp, loamy, pungent, and of cat piss. Cats prowl round in there, we see them every day, crouching, squatting, scratching up the dirt, staring out at us with their yellow eyes as if we're something they're hunting. (Margaret Atwood, *Cat's Eye*, p.74)

At a first glance this is a straightforwardly descriptive passage. Yet every signifier bears a metaphorical meaning (compare the discussion of Beryl Bainbridge's *A Quiet Life* in Chapter Six). It is also true that in excerpting the passage for study I am misrepresenting its elements: each acquires its meaning in relation to each other and within a metaphorical field that spans the length of the novel and defines the imputed memory of the protagonist, Elaine. Thus the wooden footbridge and the ravine which it crosses is a symbolic location to which the novel returns again and again, adding layers of pigment almost like a painter working in oils. On this scene is placed both the power of traumatic memory, and the potential for its resolution when at the end Elaine realises that 'There's nothing more for me to see. The bridge is only a bridge, the river a river, the sky is a sky'. (p.419). At that point she has learnt that her life need no longer be occupied by an unwanted metaphor. The bridge and the ravine have become ordinary, reminding us how the fecundity of metaphor and its nightmarish power may be inseparable. To be cured may in some ways be to find life grown duller, less resonant. For us readers, entering into the metaphor appears to constitute an important aspect of our own response: it becomes productive within our own thought and language. As a minor example, it was only after I had written the phrase about the painter above that I realised its significance: the heroine of the novel grows up to be a painter who uses her painting as her way of coming to terms with the terrors of childhood.

Let me return briefly to some elements of the passage. The proliferation of weeds (and Elaine's botanical knowledge) link us to the father, himself a biologist portrayed as a man at home in the wild. They thus locate themselves within a tame/free contrast which runs through the novel. The abundant weeds contrast with the cultivated flowers in the neat suburban gardens of Elaine's new (and treacherous) friends. The smell and texture of earth is another recurrent signifier, its metaphorical meaning linked to death and the graveyard above the ravine, and activated in plot terms at the moment later on when the girls 'pretend' to bury Elaine alive in a hole on a building plot. Smells, and the sense of smell code memory throughout the novel. Deadly nightshade brings together at least two layers of connotation. A child's fear of accidental poisoning merges with a sexual suggestion of which L.P. Hartley made use in another novel of growing up and adolescence (*The Go-Between*). The plant's botanical name is *atropa belladona*, the deathly beautiful lady, a connotation reinforced by the reference to valentine candies. In turn, as you see, the plant's dangers are menacingly hightlighted by Elaine's beautiful but deadly friend, Cordelia (her own name a reference to King Lear's third daughter). The cats may connote the feral; that which was tamed but now runs free. At all events, explicit reference to their yellow eyes points us to Elaine's treasured marble, totem against disaster and origin of the novel's title. The force of metaphors is gained not by isolated occurrences but by their recurrence and interplay through a whole text. To enumerate items as I just have is to remove them from their dynamic matrix. But this is in the good cause, I hope, of drawing attention to how even a short passage (like a short conversation) may be packed with metaphorical resonance.

So far, we have proceeded largely on the assumption of a rough equivalence between metaphor and a (paraphrased) idea. We have spoken of metaphors for argument, for ageing, and so on. Literary texts however often confront us with a kind of indeterminacy, with what is patently metaphorical utterance, but where the sense of the metaphor cannot be traced directly to an obvious referent. On such occasions our decoding skill is excited but also tantalised; we shuffle possibilities without coming to rest on one single one. So in a single poem ('The Soul has Bandaged moments') Emily Dickinson likens the soul variously to a bomb, a bee, and a captive felon, each image bringing with it an affective charge that defies straightforward paraphrase, and lures the mind in different directions. Contemplation of an object reveals itself as a dialogue between the mind's appropriation of that object for its own purposes and the irreducibility (the *thatness*) of the object itself. This is something of which the American poet William Carlos Williams was deeply aware:

THE MIND HESITANT

Sometimes the river
becomes a river in the mind
or of the mind
or in and of the mind

Its banks snow
the tide falling a dark
rim lies between
the water and the shore

And the mind hesitant
regarding the stream
senses
a likeness which it

will find — a complex
image; something
of white brows
bound by a ribbon

of sooty thought
beyond, yes well beyond
the mobile features
of swiftly

flowing waters, before
the tide will
change
and rise again, maybe

One state of mind in which to read poetry is that in which it is possible to accept the existence of a dialogue between precision and uncertainty. The need for precision arises from the attention to the obduracy of things and of language; it does not let us get away with blandness or vagueness. On the other hand, uncertainty reminds us of the existence of unpin-downable meanings, and the need to keep trying. It seems to me that this is what — reflexively, as it were — Williams' poem is about. That is the way an external object like a river is both itself and at the same time an image in the mind ('a likeness which it/ will find'), the plastic stuff of our own dreams and fantasies. Williams, it seems to me, is reflecting upon the way rivers possess a topographical specificity (the river from the standpoint of the geographer, the navigator, or civil engineer) but are also the source of a cluster of profound metaphors to do with currents, floods, bursting banks, or life as river.

Poetry, I am asserting, is a form of speech in which metaphor is likely to be displayed in all its rich ambiguity. Poems are not only semiotically highly charged themselves; attentively read they recall us to the creative power developed by the metaphors in which we think. Often, a symbol cannot just be translated into one single equivalent. Far from constituting the drawback implied in the question 'why can't she say what she means?', this movement between image and potential meaning, the pleasure in icon and the pleasure in testing possibility is precisely the kind of reading experience I am holding out as formative and necessary.

The content of this chapter almost defies the traditional closing summing up. I am very conscious that in this and the following chapter I have treated schematically, and in a linear fashion, phenomena which are better characterised by process and simultaneity. I can only hope that – like the inventories and models often used in counselling training – these schemes will be understood not as mechanical and absolute, but as tools for awareness. There are several things I want to pick up and hold onto. One is to remind that the potency of metaphor lies in its bridging of the conceptual and the affective. The other is that what gets said and heard between two people or between counsellor and client is a co-production, not a revelation of immutable truth. Metaphor is an inescapable feature of this co-production, and may constitute an arena where both can reach towards change. The arrival of a new metaphor may be the point at which a whole new conceptual scheme can be adopted. For the therapist or counsellor, the activity of reading metaphorically rich texts can constitute a form of serious and developmental play. In turn, metaphors themselves will be embedded in stories. To the framing and re-framing potential of narrative the next chapter is devoted.

SUGGESTIONS FOR FURTHER READING

Murray Cox and Alice Theilgaard (1987) *Mutative Metaphors in Psychotherapy: The Aeolian Mode.* London: Tavistock.

George Lakoff and Mark Johnson (1980) *Metaphors We Live By.* Chicago, IL: Chicago UP.

Ellen Y. Siegelbaum (1990) *Metaphor and Meaning in Psychotherapy.* New York: The Grove Press.

A.J. Soyland (1994) *Psychology as Metaphor.* London: Sage.

CHAPTER FIVE

On Narrative

In the previous chapter we reached the point of looking at metaphor in terms of re-framing and change. The argument was that since our experience is thought and talked in metaphors there is always the possibility (even while we acknowledge that some metaphors are probably too deeply embedded in fundamental human experiences to be altered) that our understanding of experience and the meanings attached to it can be re-framed by revising or altering our metaphors. Work with texts, it was argued, is one way of extending our awareness of these processes. However, it is evident that we cannot restrict the discussion of the plasticity of language to metaphor. Metaphor represents one dimension of language and thought. But to discuss it as we have is to risk minimising another fundamental dimension of discourse: that is, movement through time, the representation of processes on a temporal plane. This section, therefore, focuses on narrative, the telling of stories. There is an analogy here with the contrast established in Chapter One between the vertical (paradigmatic) and horizontal (syntagmatic) dimensions of language. Talking about metaphor in the abstract tends to imply that metaphors float free, unembedded in the forward movement of discourse. This section will attempt to redress the balance.

Let me start by telling a little story of my own. Suddenly it seems as though 'everyone' is talking about narrative. The subject seems to have become a flavour of the month, or rather of the late 1980s and early 1990s. Social scientists, psychologists, economists, even lawyers, are suddenly talking about narrative (for examples see Nash 1990, Shotter and Gergen 1989, Young 1987). Those of us who work in literature find ourselves partly flattered that an area which we have been studying for years has suddenly come to be treated as important; partly miffed at our territory being taken over, and trumpetted as though new. This chapter represents an attempt to define what narrative is, how it works, and to specify its relevance to the work in hand. The chapter that follows relates the topic more explicitly to literary texts.

Broadly, narrative is the telling of stories. This, however, is an inadequate definition, partly because of the low status accorded to 'story' which thus marginalises narrative. To put it another way, narrative is the representation of processes in time. Narrative is a moving image, a reporting of events in a sequence. While narrative speaks of time, it also normally speaks of causation, how one thing led to another. Crucial to this account of narrative is the thesis which runs through this book: that narrative is not – any more than any other form of representation – neutral, not an unmediated record, but a process of selection and organisation with rules and conventions of its own, and carried out from a particular point of view. Language, I have already suggested, is persuasive as well as referential, and the same point will be developed about narrative. To tell a story is not just to recount indisputable and already existing facts, but to put over a message. To speak of events is simultaneously to speak of values and beliefs. It is also to take part in a real or imaginary social situation: as Katherine Young (1987) points out, the 'lodgement of stories in speaking situations returns attention to the mutuality of their construction, shifting interest from monologue to dialogue' (p.14).

In the sense suggested above, narrative comprises a wide range of communicative phenomena, including television and radio news broadcasts, comic strips, and works of history and biography, as well as novels, films, and plays. Above all, I want to register that narrative is not confined to technological media (printing, broadcasting, or even script), but is a fundamental feature of everyday communication. We all of us tell stories, morning, noon, and night. In talking about neighbours, relatives, and colleagues, in telling friends and partners about our day, in talking to each other about world events, we humans constantly generate narratives, narratives which (as I hope to show) have much in common with the more formalised and highly-worked narratives we meet in novels. It is out of such narratives, out of the constant outpouring of stories to which we are subjected and in which we routinely participate that much of our sense of reality, of other people, and our common world is shaped.

This account of the ubiquity of narrative has a number of important consequences. One is that it calls into question the conventional binary distinction between truth and fiction. Narrative structures both what we believe to be fabrications, and what we conventionally hold to be 'the truth'. To say as much is not to provide a charter for lying, or to collude with a relativistic belief that any story is as good as any other, provided only that it is effective as story. It does, however, imply that the process of weighing the claims of competing stories is even more complex than often supposed, involving as it does the recognition of the narrative and rhetorical designs of the stories we hear. Truth and fiction exist on a continuum, and no messages arrive uncoded, innocent of beliefs or persuasion. Let us try to follow this through.

Underlying the argument about metaphor in the previous section was a suggestion that the metaphors we use foreground or highlight certain aspects of reality and obscure or conceal others. The same case can be made out about narrative: the story provides a framing device within which the datum or the details have meaning. If the story I tell is that social life is deteriorating and manners and standards in decline, each sighting of litter, aggressive behaviour on the streets, or rudeness from a neighbour's child will lock into place in my story. I would like to suggest that even if you do not concur with me in seeing life as unendingly mediated through stories, the re-framing device of deciphering belief in terms of story is still useful. What stories does such and such a belief require me to tell? Conversely, on what stories does this belief depend? Sometimes people's narratives will be implicit, sometimes explicit. If I am feeling aggrieved and irritated by somebody, I shall pick up details of their behaviour and weave them into a narrative which I tell myself, or indeed may tell in whole or in part to a third party. The story will focus on examples of person A's behaviour that injure me, and will almost certainly background contrary observations and possibilities (e.g. that they don't always do these things, or that irritating me has never even entered into their thoughts – or indeed that I am myself doing something which triggers them off). Fresh instances will be seized upon to develop or substantiate the point ('You know what I was saying to you the other day about A? Well, would you believe it, this morning he...'). Someone whose plot repertoire only seems to run to stories of this kind is sometimes described as 'paranoid'. But you don't have to be paranoid to make up stories. The fact that the whole of a story (unlike another sub-set of narratives, the joke) is not necessarily all told at once, should not obscure the presence of latent or elaborated narrative surrounding most or all of our observations about the world around us, or indeed about ourselves.

Telling stories is a central mode of being in the world, and a large part of what we consider as knowledge is shaped in story form. It would appear that the modalities of narrative and the modalities of memory complement and reinforce each other. This represents a development of the cognitive argument that it is much easier to remember data when we can see the point, when the data fits together in a larger scheme. That larger scheme, I am suggesting, is likely to be found to be some sort of story. Individual and social memories are carried along in narratives. Those narratives have in turn their own logic and their own momentum.

The argument that I am putting here plainly bears upon the task of listening. If what Frank Kermode (1967) once called 'the basic human task of imaginative self-invention' (p.146) is carried out in narrative, then what the therapeutic session presumably offers is the opportunity to elaborate, develop, and above all re-think your narratives. James Hillman (1983) forcibly argues not only that the Freudian case-history is a brilliant piece of fiction-making in a therapeutic genre, but that analyst and analysand collaborate in a mutual fiction.

> The force of diagnostic stories cannot be exaggerated. Once one has been written into a particular clinical fantasy with its expectations, its typicalities, its character traits, and the rich vocabulary it offers for recognizing oneself, one then begins to recapitulate one's life into the shape of the story. One's past too is retold and finds a new internal coherence, even inevitability, through this abnormal story. A diagnosis is indeed a *gnosis*: a mode of self-knowledge that creates a cosmos in its image. (pp.14–15 and Chapter One generally)

Telling your story can (to make a Winnicott-like point) be a way of detoxifying experience. By implication, anyone who offers another their undivided attention is offering space for story-making, and the more the therapist knows about stories, and the larger repertoire of elements to which he or she has access, the better.

Although they do not in fact use literary examples, this is the point of White and Epston's (1990) book *Narrative Means to Therapeutic Ends*. They conceive of life and relationships in relation to the writing and reading of texts, and point to all that can be backgrounded or thrust out of sight by the dominant story. Thus they quote Edward Bruner:

> Narrative structures organize and give meaning to experience, but there are always feelings and lived experience not fully encompassed by the dominant story. (p.10)

There is an exact parallel with the account of metaphor given in the last section. For White and Epston the making of new stories, and the achievement of less problem-saturated accounts is a central function of family therapy in particular. Stories are transformative, and people need to learn to become the authors as well as the subjects of their own stories.

If we provisionally grant a case of this sort, we need to move on to ask what the characteristics of narrative are. So far I have made do with general reference to storytelling and to representations in time. A large part of this section and the chapter which follows will be given to filling out details, but we need some kind of preliminary grasp on the subject. To what phenomena does my rather cavalier use of the term 'narrative' refer? Two complementary things come to mind. In everyday terms I could call them selection and shaping. The two activities interpenetrate each other. To tell a story you have to select (generally at a subliminal level) from the infinite number of things you could have said, and the choice will largely be dictated by considerations of form. Stories are both required to explain something, and to be attractively told, hence the need to attend to the rhetorical heightening of detail. It is widely felt to be more impressive, if you are accounting for your late arrival, to say that the 'phone hasn't stopped ringing all morning, rather than that you had two 'phone calls, and that in any case you hadn't left yourself sufficient time for the journey.

So my first point is that narratives are governed by form, and that these forms are cultural and (usually) learned at an early age. Tellers and listeners are apt to share conventions about what makes a good story. These will include criteria for the relevance of details, about the rhetorical heightening of detail by exaggeration, about avoiding overmuch repetition or digression, above all about endings. It is crucial that a narrative be felt to be going somewhere, towards a denouement, a revelation, a punchline, an explanation for an enigma, some sort of closure, even if that closure is only temporary, a 'to be continued next week/next time we meet'. Stories which just add one episode to another, one item to the next are widely felt to be ill-formed and boring, as parents and teachers often feel about children's stories. Narrative needs to be going somewhere. Which leads me to my next stage.

For it is a crucial convention that narrative needs to have a point (the worst thing that can happen to some one who tells a story, says the American linguist William Labov, is if the interlocutor says 'so what?'). Stories embody messages; they are told so as to prove something to yourself, if to nobody else. Stories are rarely if ever told just out of the blue or about random subjects: they are told because they seem to document a case, demonstrate a truth, prove a point, or create solidarity with the person you are speaking to. The messages can, of course, be of all sorts, and need not necessarily be those consciously intended by the speaker. We shall be coming back to some varieties of message in due course. Meanwhile what I want to emphasise is this purposive dimension of narrative. Messages can be latent or overt. 'The point is this' my grandfather would say as he neared the goal of his story; but at other times hearers are left to work out for themselves what it was all in aid of. But whether latent or overt, the message is there, and the details fitted into a framework that confirms that message. In the first chapter I argued that language was rhetorical and persuasive, and the same point must be made in relation to narrative. Narrative is performative; we tell stories to have an effect on our hearers or on ourselves. 'It took me eight hours to get home from London, and the bloody buffet was closed' is a portion of narrative designed to elicit sympathy from the hearer, and may well be developed in the direction of a failure of transport story ('British Rail!'), or a story about the self ('these things always happen to me'/'just my luck'; or 'I've been let down again').

But I must re-iterate something I said earlier. To stress that stories are told for effect, and that the demands of coherence and effectiveness govern how the story is told and even the choice of elements is not meant to imply that people spend their time lying. But it does imply that part of being an alert listener is developing an ear for narrative and its messages, and recognising that what we are told needs to be checked against the demands of the genre and the occasion as well as the demands of abstract truth. Faced by somebody's statement – about their family, their neighbours, the people in the next street, or themselves – we need to ask ourselves 'in what sort of story does this statement figure?' Stories are shaped not alone by the pressure of the events they recount, but by the social structure and transferential pressures of the occasions on which they are told. Todorov (1984) helpfully summarises Bakhtin:

> In their analyses, Freud and his disciples always tend to play up individual motivations... but aren't the words of the patient, uttered during the analytic session, determined as well, if not more, by the interaction that comes into being in the microsociety formed by the physician and the patient...? [He then quotes Bakhtin himself] What is reflected in these verbal utterances is not the dynamics of the individual soul, but the *social dynamics* of the interrelations of doctor and patient. [Todorov continues:]... Bakhtin would even say that it is not the relation patient-physician that results from transference... but rather that the reverse occurs: memories are interpreted in the light of the structure of the present occasion. [Bakhtin, argues Todorov, is not rejecting but reinterpreting Freud when he asks:] Would it not be more correct to say that the physician and the patient, having joined forces, are doing nothing but projecting into the unconscious complex... their present relations...? (pp.31–2)

Narratives, then, are relational, and have to be understood in performative terms. What is the message of this story, and what effect does it seek to have upon me? How does its point shape its contents?

Once having located storytelling in an interpersonal transaction, we need to return to the formal elements of story. Let us begin with time. One of the ways in which narrative makes its status as representation most clear, its difference from reality most distinct, is in the nature of its time bounds. Stories impose beginnings, middles, and ends upon their subject matter. They also take their own time. Students of narrative generally distinguish between two levels. One level is that of the telling (sometimes referred to as discourse), the other that of the subject matter. Located in an interpersonal and social world, these become Katherine Young's 'Taleworld' and 'Storyrealm'. The shaping of the discourse in time has a complex and always richly significant relationship to the time sequence of the represented events. Broadly, the former will only have a loose relationship with the latter.

Attention to the representation of process in time is one way of becoming aware of the formal demands of story. Obviously an inventory of those formal demands is out of the question here, but it is perhaps possible to give some sense of the formulaic element of narrative. By 'formulae' I refer to the existence of a cultural stock of sayings, and of standard devices which are used in the making of stories, and indeed often figure as proto-narratives of their own. Such formulae may comprise little plots, akin to proverbs, and may indeed provide a structuring motif for a larger story. Crucially, they express deeply-seated beliefs. Take, for example, the formulae of what you might call 'subject-centred causation', those that advance a more or less overt belief that what happens to people is in a large measure a product of their own personality and acts: 'she's been asking for it for a long time' (said with grim satisfaction); 'he got himself thrown off the committee'; 'he had it coming to him'; or, the converse 'she didn't deserve that.' These are the sort of thing I mean when I speak of structuring formulae. They simultaneously mobilise beliefs about human nature and organise the data of the story into sense, endowing events with meaning. They may become recurrent motifs in a larger story.

Another sort of formula asserts impersonal causation, suggesting a world governed by large metaphysical forces, fate perhaps. 'It was bound to happen', 'it had to happen', 'it was meant to happen', 'if it isn't one thing it's another', 'it would have happened sooner or later', 'there's always a first time' and the like. Highly sophisticated narratives, too, are built upon such generative motifs, even if they are not always spelled out. Sometimes the formulae employed are reflexive in the sense that they draw attention to the dimension of telling. 'Story of my life' some one will say, ruefully adding another instance to the chronicle of things that have gone wrong. 'Spoke too soon, didn't I' alludes to a superstitious belief in the danger of uttering hopes or touching on good fortune. Such elements (and their number is legion) may provide local structure or indeed structure for a whole tale. In this they are very similar to motifs, that is to say the seeds or kernels of stories.

We may see stories as generated by the interaction of narrative kernels with the demands of the telling. Stories of typification hide behind statements like 'just the sort of thing she *would* do', or 'I wish you wouldn't always...', or '*typical*'. These, like the stories people tell about themselves, are based upon plot motifs, core assertions demonstrated by the subsequent development. Another generative item can displace responsibility from the speaker to another person – 'he makes me sick'. Many tales can be generated from motifs like', 'it's what I deserve', or 'she's always had it in for me', and one route for listening as for criticism is to look for the underlying repertoire of motifs (a subject acutely drawn with absorbing detail by Cox and Theilgaard (1987), especially Chapters One, Three, Nine, and Ten). It would, however, be too simple to see a single motif lying at the bottom of every story. Stories may also be generated from the contradiction between two motifs, and it appears to me that stories are indeed one of the most common ways of attempting to resolve the cognitive dissonance generated by our preferred plots.

While at one level stories are the elaborate working out of underlying problems, we have also to look for tropes, the organising formulae in which the story takes shape. A trope is an organising convention, a culturally acceptable figure of speech which provides us with a ready-made form in which to say things. One of the most common narrative tropes in English-speaking cultures is one or other form of irony. This crops up in all sorts of ways, for instance in conjunction with negative tag questions such as 'He had to put his big foot in it, didn't he?', where the listener is drawn into compliance with this observation upon the gap between the real and the ideal. 'It would happen to me' is another faintly humorous way of alluding to a half-formulated belief in the adversity of the universe. Whole situations can be encompassed through the ironic trope: 'I bought these new boots in March and of course it hasn't rained since'; 'I went all the way over the other side of town and they were closed, of course'. The ironies of situation and fate bulk large in day-to-day discourse. Yet irony can never be a formal property alone: it implies a complicity between speaker and listener over the head of the subject matter. As a narrative trope irony speaks of both a way of coping with the difficulties of living and a relationship with the interlocutor based on a wry superiority. Both of you share an implicit overview of events – 'Have to see the funny side, don't you'. A whole story can consist of a demonstration of the ironic propensities of things. Events, teller, and listener exist in a mutually referring triangle. Irony modalises the speaker's relationship both to events and to the listener.

So narratives embody a variety of structuring features. They give meaningful disposition to energies and emotions which might otherwise be unmanageable. There is an analogy, it is often pointed out, between the structure of a sentence and the structure of a narrative. One is, so to speak, a much bigger version of the other. The analogy points towards the possibility of devising a grammar of narrative on the lines of the grammar of a sentence, with its elements taking up roles within it. The 'existents' (characters and things) would thus be equivalent to nouns; actions and events to verbs; descriptions to modifiers. The analogy helps us to understand the roles which the various participants in a narrative occupy and the relationships established between them. Characters, things, places are present, the analogy asserts, not for their intrinsic merits or characteristics, but because they fulfil the needs of a particular narrative. Thus we are likely to find actors who do things (as it were the grammatical subject of transactive verbs), and actors to whom things are done. We find that some states of affairs seem to just happen, and others to be brought about by human agency.

Characters are relational, in the sense that their roles exist in complementary relations with other roles. Not only do they need to be seen as a group rather than an assembly of individuals, but they have to be seen as occupying structural positions in relation to the needs of the story. There is, I have argued elsewhere (Knights 1992), an analogy between the cast of a novel and the members of a group. The figure of the villain is a case in point. Many narratives seem to require a figure to carry all the evil, all the negative potential that haunts the plot. Let me make it clear that I am not implying that people are *not* from time to time mischievous, obstructive, self-interested or even downright wicked: just that the figure of the villain often serves to locate all that is wrong in one place, thereby evading the necessity of taking a long look at the whole system within which injustice and injury occur. Just as the villain of the piece acts as a carrier for all the hostility the story engenders (thereby exonerating others from their share of blame), so other figures receive other emotions appropriate to the nature of the tale (victim, innocent, rebel, the one who will not be put down, the voice of commonsense, and so on). A narrative is a complex economy which both engenders and manages the emotions roused in tellers and listeners by the telling.

Even apparently mimetic or realistic tales do more than describe: they propose a system of rules for constituting meanings. Such rules – which find their analogue in the norms which a group generates – are the basis on which an interlocutor gets drawn into the mental world of the storyteller. A listener is not asked just to hear (or dispute) 'the facts'. He or she is implicitly invited to share a set of norms about how the facts may be interpreted. A story domain rigidly organised into goodies and baddies, a tale of injury and revenge, or a recurrent plot-line where the teller is the triumphant hero of his own tale, incite us to go on expecting or inventing stories with the same structuring rules.

Just as characters and objects provide the nouns of our tale, so plot can be seen as equivalent to the verbs. I have been offering an account of the 'existents' in terms of their roles within the whole economy of the tale. Let me now touch briefly on the dynamics of story. Anything I say here is likely to seem rather schematic, and I should emphasise that no story assumes anything like a standard shape. Oral stories especially are likely to be oblique; sketchy yet repetitive. They are also less likely to be self-contained, depending for their meaning upon other narratives previous, or to come. Nevertheless, narrative does have certain requirements which can be glimpsed in oral as well as written narratives. At the level of content there is a movement from one state of affairs to another, the process of change often involving a dramatic reversal. At the level of telling there is an overall movement from things hidden (a secret only known to the teller, an enigma, a gap in knowledge) to revelation or the clearing up of mystery. Frequently this journey involves suspense, the balancing of the hearer's desire to know against the pleasurable sensation of waiting. The narrative manages the unfolding relationship between knowledge and ignorance, satisfaction and frustration, timing its outcomes to satisfy both the desire to prolong waiting and the desire to find out. In terms of the relation between the teller and the listener the pattern of withholding or disclosure can be seen as an exercise of power – the power accruing from possession of a secret which some one else wants to know.

Much discomfort may be generated in the listener by the ins and outs of narrative. So the provision of a clearly signalled conclusion is one of the chief elements in people's sense of a well-formed story, a sense that has often been teased and held up to question in twentieth-century novels. Suspense, on the other hand, is likely to be more highly developed in a written tale, since oral stories tend to work more through accumulation, and a succession of small climaxes. Also, of course, the rhetoric of the telling can be finely tuned to the hearer's response if the story is being told aloud. The narrative is also more likely to be contextualised, building reference to the common situation in which teller and listener find themselves. Nevertheless, the movement from mystery to disclosure via an element of delay informs most kinds of narrative. And as the pattern of disclosure continues, it generates the need for the figures hinted at above.

While bearing in mind the social theatre which novels and their like enact, and while affirming that oral and written narratives throw light upon each other, it is necessary at the same time to acknowledge the differences. It is not only that written narratives are likely to be more highly worked than oral ones. The crucial difference resides in the relations between the author, the audience and the context. Not only is the written narrative much less dependent upon its immediate context than the spoken, but for obvious reasons the author cannot (even in serial publication where some responsiveness to audience reception is possible) take such account of the way his/her story is going down with the audience. Feedback, if it occurs at all, is much delayed, and the initial audience, that present at the point of writing, is an imaginary one. Nevertheless, printed tales, too, exist in relation to readers, demand certain types of reading, meet with resistance or compliance. Although the prime subject matter of the next chapter concerns texts that would normally be counted as 'literature', I hope that what is said here will turn out to have a bearing as well upon the oral narratives of everyday life. Informing this chapter (as indeed the book as a whole) are the twin notions that central to what counselling and psychotherapy have to offer to their clients is the opportunity to invent languages to speak change. And that what in turn fictions have to offer counsellors and their like is a repertoire of narrative resources.

In the chapter which follows we shall develop some of these themes further in relation to prose fiction. I hope that what is said there will both feed back into an understanding of the narratives of everyday life, and lead the reader on into engagement with fictions which – among other things – serve the function of enlarging the repertoire of scripts and types on which they draw. Telling is not simply a report on experience, but a productive making of meanings which foregrounds some meanings and conceals others. It is a social and dialogic procedure with its own rules and own dynamics.

SUGGESTIONS FOR FURTHER READING

Frank Kermode (1967) *The Sense of an Ending: Studies in the Theory of Fiction.* London: Oxford University Press.

Cristopher Nash (ed) (1990) *Narrative in Culture: The Uses of Storytelling in the Sciences, Philosophy and Literature.* London: Routledge.

Shlomith Rimmon-Kenan (ed) (1987) *Discourse in Psychoanalysis and Literature.* London: Methuen.

Shlomith Rimmon-Kenan (1983) *Narrative Fiction: Contemporary Poetics.* London: Methuen.

John Shotter and Kenneth Gergen (eds) (1989) *Texts of Identity.* London: Sage.

Jeremy Tambling (1991) *Narrative and Ideology.* Buckingham: Open University Press.

Michael White and David Epston (1990) *Narrative Means to Therapeutic Ends.* New York: W.W. Norton.

Katherine Galloway Young (1987) *Taleworlds and Storyrealms: the Phenomenology of Narrative.* Dordrecht: Martinus Nijhoff.

CHAPTER SIX

Interactive Reading II
Novels and Stories

The preceding chapter sketched a theory of narrative with the aim of bringing together in a single perspective the phenomena of both spoken and written storytelling. We now turn our attention back to a sub-division of the realm of narrative, that constituted by prose fiction. I am here employing, as I pointed out at the beginning of Chapter Three, a somewhat arbitrary division between the subject matter of that chapter and of this. The emphasis here is on novels and short stories and how they simulate biography and social relations. After the generalisations of the last chapter, it will be necessary to draw on some quite specific material. In this chapter we survey some of the attributes and working modes of fiction, and ways in which fiction may be read. In the next, we take a particular novel and use it to demonstrate a reading of a text.

MADE UP WORLDS

This chapter as a whole is trying to gather up a number of themes (interpretation, symbolism, metaphor, and so on) that have run through the book as a whole, and direct them towards an exploration of the kind of activity involved in the critical reading of novels and stories. To that extent the procedure is cumulative. Much of what was said about the active reading of poetry applies as well to reading prose fiction. But the difference of extent – the sheer size of a novel – brings its own kind of problems. In a sense a quantitative difference becomes a qualitative one: the protraction of the reading experience through time involves us with a greater range of structural features. A prolonged narrative speaks of events, linking one event with another into what we know as a plot. Different kinds of novel vary in the degree and complexity of plot, although broadly speaking the novel which concentrates on consciousness and the inner details of experience is less eventful, and fosters cohesion through continuity of thematic material rather than through the suspenseful and surprising linkage of one event with another. Either way, readers develop a vicarious memory as they read. And any prolonged narrative requires of us varying patterns of attention.

Before turning to the formal properties of fiction, I want to emphasise something about the theatre of the novel. We all tend to read novels in a psychologising spirit. So indeed do many novels offer themselves to be read: as studies of human experience, motivation, and behaviour where the locus of attention is the individual, the family, or intimate relationships. However, to a greater or lesser degree (very strongly in the case of the realist tradition) fictions also offer another, complementary, reading. That is as models of societies in action, with all the networks, connections, economic and class relationships that life in society involves. It is especially true of the great realists (in English terms such writers as Dickens, George Eliot, Hardy) that all the time they embed character and personal relations in a large and dynamic social world. It would be a very one-sided appropriation of their work to read them solely in psychological terms.

Let us return to the narrative impulse, the impulse gratified both by telling and listening to stories. Partly this represents a desire to shape, to form, to explain, to give pattern and coherence to experience. Yet fictions (and I have already pointed out that we cannot place a radical break between 'truth' and 'fictions') also bring a further satisfaction: they have an even freer rein in bringing about desirable states of affairs. Thus we may well see novels, drama, films as fantasies, but fantasies which have become sharable, through being brought out into the light of the public world. Fantasy, of course, is characterised by the malleability, the plasticity of its subject matter. Can we classify as fantasies even those fictions that propose the greatest fidelity to the obdurate materiality of the world? I think we need to push forward a little bit the consideration of the relations of fantasy and mimesis (the attempt to represent a known and sharable world).

In Chapter Two we looked briefly at the subject of fantasy in connection with the making of fictions. There I pointed out that fantasies could be both private to the individual and at the same time social. Individuals can entertain fantasies, indeed may well spend a good deal of their time fantasising; but not only are there also collective fantasies about the nature of the world (as in one social group's ideas about another group), but the very forms and languages of individual fantasy are themselves largely socially given. Fantasy is not as entirely private as we often suppose. Unconscious energy gets attached to signifiers which are in their nature public. I am trying to get at a paradox of sorts: that fantasy exhibits the potential both for liberation and repression. Liberation in that in fantasy the mind can break free from the present limitations of material existence; repression, through the treadmill effect by which fantasy and daydream are committed to repetition of a narrow range of themes, and also because of the very power of the emotional charge with which fantasy becomes invested. A belief is, so to speak, held in place by an investment of emotional energy. It is hard to get at or shift the structure of emotion or fantasy on which the belief rests (which is partly the reason why people are so rarely convinced by arguments – even those whose justice they grant). Beliefs are all the stronger for being locked in place by irrational fantasies. All the contradictory evidence with which life presents us can be translated to fulfil personal or communal mythic requirements. By inviting our participation at the level where fantasy and rationality intersect, fiction enables us to question the reciprocal relations between wishes and belief. Thus, while a good deal of fiction can be seen in terms of wish-fulfilment (rewarding the just, punishing the guilty, bringing sundered lovers together) or as the symbolic resolution of historical conflicts (resolving the conflict between antagonistic groups), the option is given us of resisting the pressure towards buying in to this fulfilment. Fictions may instead invite us to reflect on how our wishes and our beliefs about the real intertwine. Crucially, they offer us not galleries of frozen characters or static events, but representations of change and development, images for the processes of becoming.

While one recurrent theme of this book has been the persuasive and interpersonal nature of representations, another has been the accretion of meanings that attaches to any set of signifiers. It is the latter we need to pick now. We have spoken of illusionism, the text that seeks to persuade that it represents something that has 'really' happened. Such a text invokes criteria of plausibility (yes, we assent, I believe that these humans would behave like that), but also codes the real world through a freight of objects, those details of places and things which conjure up scenes. In this view, then, details (the layout of a house, the furnishings of a room, the arrival of a train, the streets of Manchester or of Johannesburg) may work either or both mimetically, to establish verisimilitude, or symbolically. We are moving towards questions to do with the implication of detail in a larger structure. For an item (an object, a repeated action) can come to press upon our consciousness as carrying a value in the story that exceeds its merely circumstantial importance, and so draw attention to a field of possible meanings within the text as a whole. The term for the use of an item as an example of or an element of some larger set of objects is metonymy. Unlike metaphor – where an unlike term stands for something else – metonyny exhibits an element which is part of something else or represents a larger class of similar objects. It is the characteristic mode of the realist novel.

Let us look at a passage from a novel by Beryl Bainbridge as an example of a text in a realistic register.

> Alan took the morning off school, to go into town to be measured for his new suit. It meant clean underpants and a vest. He was defiant about the expense involved and the expression on his mother's face when the teachers told her, new suit or not, he was unlikely to pass his examinations. He huddled against the station fence, watching the men in the yard shovelling coal into stiff sacks. The slack glittered under a layer of frost. At this hour there were only a few businessmen on the platform – father

had dawdled over his telephone calls before leaving the house, and it was gone ten o'clock. In the spring the station was circled by alder bushes and pussy willow; the buds thrust fat and creamy through the palings of the fence. Now the trees leaned inland, ripped by the wind blowing across the bleak uncultivated fields. The rose trees by the Gentlemen's toilet were pruned, black and mutilated, a foot above the frozen ground. It might have been Siberia, he thought, save for the council offices and the red-brick houses built in a half-moon beyond the coal yards. (*A Quiet Life*, Chapter Four)

Here the details (a suburban railway station, northern England, 1945) are less innocent than they may have appeared: look again. 'The rose trees by the Gentlemen's toilet were pruned, black and mutilated, a foot above the frozen ground'. The novel is full of things stunted, pruned. The word 'mutilated' itself is a giveaway. Alan's father, an amateur gardener of the obsessive school, has his fatal heart attack after an unsuccessful attempt to saw down a sycamore tree. The lexical field so defined is contiguous with another which has to do with impeded action, constraint. The physical not having room to move without hitting yourself describes Alan and Madge's home literally and metaphorically. Physical constraint shades into psychological restraint. Everywhere the characters turn there is the risk of breaking something, and the danger of breaking a physical object (the wireless, perched precariously on a ledge; the front room clock) codes the fragility of the human relations lived within that setting. The cold house in which there is no room to move is both a representation of a physical place, and a metaphor.

The point of this example (which could be paralleled time and again) is that part of the process of reading is to become attuned to the profusion of textual indicators which between them weave the meanings of the narrative. We are talking about repetition and cohesion. Repetition because the recurrence of an object, a particular kind of event, or an image creates significance, cohesion because such items frequently fall into kinship patterns, organising a story over time. It is the inferential work we do as readers as we process these patterns that enables us both to make sense at a surface level and to decipher the inner story within the outer story.

The patterns of kinship between textual items are not simply of the surface, a matter of decoration. They are deeply embedded in the structures underlying the whole narrative. In a word, they are thematic, where the word 'theme' speaks of a problematic, a contradictory or an urgent feature of experience to which the narrative repeatedly returns. We have already touched on the relational roles of characters within the structure of events, and to this subject (as much else) we shall return in the next chapter. My point for the moment is that characters, objects and events figure in patterns of relationship and contrast to each other. Frequently, these are binary patterns, where two sets of items occur in an unfolding contrast to one another. So, in *A Quiet Life*, indoors and outdoors, the garden and the wood on the way to the beach, heat and cold, suburb and city, form a binary set, which is associated at the same time with Alan and his sister Madge. Binary oppositions provide a structuring principle for narrative and can as well act at the level of the human participants as at that of inanimate objects (the characters as well as the objects and places work together as contrasts). In the dynamic tension between these pairs of opposites are generated the arguments about values which underlie any text.

It is sometimes said that a writer takes bits of the real world and re-arranges them, creating a lifelike picture of the world. By this stage in the book, we should see why this account with its reification of experience won't altogether do. But it does signal both the element of play (moving things and people around), and the force of illusionism. I think that fictions may be plausibly understood in the light of the interplay between fantasy on the one hand and the obligations of socially-defined mimesis on the other. Thus a given text is likely to establish its own norm on the fantasy–mimesis continuum. Contrast this, for example, with the 'realistic' Beryl Bainbridge.

> And [the dancers] stopped, all at once, so that the skirts swirled about their legs. And, as they did so, every woman and girl and girl child in the place stood up and ran from their benches out into the space with the dancers. And now Al.Ith saw that the western side of the great hall had been carefully removed at about two-thirds of the way up, to give a view of the mountains of Zone Three from one end to the other. Here the tops were not visible, but even so, this crowd of women, lifting up their arms and performing some act of worship or of remembrance, had to bend back their heads to see the mountains. It was early evening, the light hung there with a sad and meaningful density and Al.Ith, amazed, realized that for all the time she had been shut up... with the king, she had not once gone out to gaze up at her own realm, at her own mountain heights. (Doris Lessing, *The Marriages between Zones Three, Four, and Five* pp.167–8)

Here, numerous indicators (the removal of the side of the hall. the ritualistic viewing of the mountains, the names – Al.Ith, Zone Three) suggest a realm which is not precisely 'the everyday'. Such a passage connotes the strange – the mystical, even. Texts, I suggest, establish their own norms about how they negotiate the opposing claims of mimesis and fantasy. They also map themselves onto a repertoire of communicative norms. So it is that the passage just quoted could be placed as belonging to a particular genre – here futuristic fiction. It is likely that – whether we are conscious of the process or not – we do sort communicative situations into genres, and tune our own participation accordingly (a counselling session, for example, belongs to a different genre from a conversation between friends, and both from an adult education evening class).

What is commonly found to be shocking and disturbing is where a text appears to violate the norms it has itself established. Many readers have been troubled by Melanie finding a severed hand in the kitchen drawer in *The Magic*

Toyshop, by the flood which resolves the plot of *The Mill on the Floss*, or by the statue coming to life at the end of *The Winter's Tale*. Such episodes attract a lot of unfavourable critical commentary, as also does the proliferation of coincidence in many otherwise realistic novels. I suggest that we may learn from this affront: such irruptions through the smooth surface, such breakings down of illusion may indeed be growth points, the points where we learn most about the work of symbolisation, and the gravitational attraction of fantasies that refuse the strait-jacket of commonsense.

Moments where communicative norms collide force us to reconsider the nature of our collaboration in the making of meanings. Do we put our own constructive effort into the stereotype, into the normal, so overlooking the surprising, inconsistent, or shocking? There is a smoothing off effect in the listening, as in the telling, of stories, and much contemporary theory has taught us to look to the breaks, the discontinuities, the sudden turns and implausibilities of texts as the points where our reading is most stretched, most challenged to reconsider its own habits. There is, it appears to me, a clear therapeutic implication. Fictions may awaken us to much we need to know about the tensions within tales, the irruption through the organised surface of things we did not mean to say, or things we did not want to hear. The material may often be too much for the structuring devices by which we propose to organise it. So a story (and, reciprocally, our attention to a story) is apt to move back and forth between the pressures exerted by the subject matter and those exerted by the requirements of structure and coherence.

NARRATION

One of the themes of the chapter on narrative was that narration is sited in interpersonal space, and subject to the gravitational forces that such a positioning implies. The needs of the communicative situation make their presence felt in the substance and manner of what gets said. While printed texts do indeed differ in many respects from spoken narrative, yet it makes sense to see them as operating within a nexus of relationships, including the relationships between readers and readings, and that between the narrative voice of the text on one hand and the community of readers on the other. This is not the appropriate place to elaborate on the historical conditions which influence both texts and readings. I neverthe-less want to make it clear that texts are not solely produced by the genius of authors, but by the author working under quite specific historical conditions and constraints, and subsequently published, distributed, known about or studied through quite material institutional structures. In an oral metaphor, the audibility of stories does not depend upon the loudness of the storyteller's voice, but upon the existence and predisposition of an audience, the provision of amplifying equipment, and the levels of background noise. This metaphor of voice provides a way in to the subject of narration.

Subject matter and form are mutually influential and both inhabit (and make reference to) a narrative context shaped by the social relatedness between teller and listener and by institutional pressures. From these generalities, I want now to pick out some elements which bear upon written fictions. First of all I want to try to get a grip upon this matter of narration. By this I refer to all those features of the text that constitute the telling, and which establish us readers in a relationship with something that we hear as the 'voice' of the story. It is a formal but important point that the voice we identify as 'the voice of the book' should never simply be identified with the voice of the author as such. The author that the text implies may well be a *persona* or guise of the author, but the identity of the historical and the implied author should never be automatically assumed. Close analysis can often locate an author's recurrent concerns, but these may be at variance both with the explicit values and beliefs of the author concerned and with other voices within the text. As we read, we need to bear in mind the nature of the relations with the reader that the text establishes, and the kind of reading it calls for. This awareness is necessary because it actually frees us as readers from the bonds which texts establish, giving us room to negotiate our own patterns of reading.

What do I mean by the 'voice' of the story, or by suggesting that we readers enter into a relationship with the narrator? Let us try to reach this through some examples. Sometimes the presence of a narrator is very clearly marked: this is the case with novels and stories written in the first person, where we have passed off on us the pretence that we are being addressed by a 'real' person who is telling us about their own experience. Presumably because of the imaginative homology we are able to intuit between ourselves as the tellers of stories and other speakers of stories, we are apt to identify with the first person narrators of novels: fictive autobiography draws us in to its experience in a very direct way:

> Cordelia and I are riding on the streetcar, going downtown, as we do on winter Saturdays. The streetcar is muggy with twice-breathed air and the smell of wool. Cordelia sits with nonchalance, nudging me with her elbow now and then, staring blankly at the other people with her grey-green eyes, opaque and glinting as metal. She can outstare anyone, and I am almost as good. We're impervious, we scintillate, we are thirteen. (Atwood, *Cat's Eye* p.4)

Such first person narrators, we can believe in the corner of our minds, are not only speaking to us, they are voicing fictive selves that we can temporarily adopt. They have other realistic attributes too. For example, unlike the traditional third person narrator, they have no access to other characters' minds except through the 'lifelike' channels of listening and observation, nor — obviously — can they see things that happen when they themselves are not present. First person narration is especially effective in creating our assent to a fictive reality precisely because it appears to give us direct access to authoritative experience (this happened to me, the one who is telling you), and because of the implied presence of the narrator within the reader's hearing. A related method of establishing the verisimilitude of the story is the framing device of some one who claims really to have been present, even if they were not necessarily the main actor in events (e.g. Conrad's Marlow or Lockwood and Nellie Dean in *Wuthering Heights*).

While first person narration foregrounds the narrator, it has no monopoly upon narrative voice. Third person texts come in a wide variety of forms, and they too embed narrators. These may or may not be characters or actors in the plot, but some are more prominent than others. For example, a narrator may, in addition to telling the story, also command a register where (s)he does a lot of explaining, generalising, and reflecting, putting the reader in the picture, guiding the reader's judgement towards appropriate things to think, revealing the true motives or guiding principles of characters, and even engaging in wide-ranging generalisations about human nature and social life. This was a well-developed tradition among the great realist novelists of the nineteenth century, and clearly exercised Andrew Davies when he came to write the screenplay for the BBC dramatisation of *Middlemarch*. Here is a passage from another of George Eliot's novels.

> Mr Dempster, on the Thursday morning, was in one of his best humours, and though perhaps some of the good-humour might result from the prospect of a lucrative and exciting bit of business in Mr Armstrong's probable lawsuit, the greater part of it was doubtless due to those stirrings of the more kindly, healthy sap of human feeling, by which goodness tries to get the upper hand in us whenever it seems to have the slightest chance – on Sunday mornings, perhaps, when we are set free from the grinding hurry of the week, and take the little three-year-old on our knee at breakfast to share our egg and muffin; in moments of trouble, when death visits our roof or when illness makes us dependent on the tending hand of a slighted wife; in quiet talks with an aged mother, of the days when we stood at her knee with our first picture-book, or wrote her loving letters from school. In the man whose childhood has known caresses there is always a fibre of memory that can be touched to gentle issues, and Mr Dempster, whom you have hitherto seen only as the orator of the Red Lion, and the drunken tyrant of a dreary midnight home, was the first-born darling son of a fair little mother. ('Janet's Repentance' in *Scenes of Clerical Life*)

Here, the narrator (who claims to be male, and relates to the reader on that basis) not only knows more about Mr Dempster than other characters in the story or indeed he himself probably could, but also places what is happening (the stirring of 'healthy sap') generically, within a theory about human nature, a theory which is exemplified (taking the little three-year-old on our knee), and based upon the memory of childhood caresses. This kind of narration looks after the reader, taking him or her earnestly into its confidence, and in so doing tending to impose its own interpretations. Another kind of narration leaves it largely up to the reader how to interpret and account for the events of the story, the narrator refusing the opportunity of providing a voice over, and restricting themselves to recording events.

However, it should be obvious by this stage that even a reticent narrator is not absent, but merely camouflaged, influencing the reader's response through the selection of detail, through stylistic choices, and the selection of what we are allowed to know about the characters' minds. In any fiction, the narrative voice is at the least an implied presence, a voice of judgment, an authority which holds potentially fissiparous strands together.

POINT OF VIEW

Any listener knows how powerful perspective can be, how characters and events take on the hue of a particular telling. Fictions offer us alternative perspectives, reinforcing our capacity to move in and out of the perspective presented to us. If it is in first person narration that our illusion of presence is strongest, by the same token it is perhaps in first person narration that we are most likely to be taken in by the narrator upon whom we lean. Since, as I suggested above, readers are inclined to identify with first person narrators we tend to suppose that they are totally honest with us, and not only honest but entirely self-aware. So it is salutary to be reminded that first person narrators too can be economical with the truth, or indeed unreliable, mistaken or misleading about the nature of their own experience. This is not a merely formal point: presumably, our desire for a narrator who both tells all and is entirely trustworthy is based upon a fantasy that our own self is unitary, just in its judgments, and available all the time to our own scrutiny. 'We all have identity crises', remarks James Hillman (1983), 'because a single identity is an illusion' (p.39), and there is therefore insight to be gained into our own self-telling when we acknowledge that first person narrators may leave in their work traces of alternative narratives which in turn point towards the possibility of alternative selves.

Take the huge holes left in her own story by Lucy Snowe, the narrator of Charlotte Brontë's last novel, *Villette*. These speak eloquently of the repressions and exclusions necessitated by her chosen life strategy – one of coping with disappointment and with the rebuffs of a male-oriented world by armouring herself against emotion. When we find that she has misled us about a significant step in the story (the stage at which she recognised the attractive Dr John as her childhood friend Graham, now grown up), the effect is not just to throw her narration and her self-awareness into doubt, but to force us to confront questions about the self as a figure in its own narratives. Lucy Snowe is a mask for her author, but the biographical reference points not only towards the biographical 'facts' about Charlotte Brontë, but outwards towards the problems inhering in biographical narrative itself: the naming of its own subject (the 'I' of the story), its ignorance and self-division, its need for both concealment and display, how it is to handle the interplay of what I knew then, and what I know now. Let us look for a few minutes at a passage where Lucy has decided to reply to Graham's letter with two letters ('one for my own relief, the other for Graham's perusal').

> To begin with: Feeling and I turned Reason out of doors, drew against her bar and bolt, then we sat down, spread our paper, dipped in the ink an eager pen, and with deep enjoyment, poured out our sincere heart. When we had done – when two sheets were covered with the language of a strongly-adherent affection, a rooted and active gratitude – (once for all, in this parenthesis, I disclaim, with the utmost scorn, every sneaking suspicion of what are called 'warmer feelings': women do not entertain these 'warmer feelings' where, from the commencement, through the whole progress of an acquaintance, they have never once been cheated of the conviction that to do so would be to commit a moral absurdity: nobody ever launches into Love unless he has seen or dreamed the rising of Hope's star over Love's troubled waters) – when, then, I had given expression to a closely-clinging and deeply-honouring attachment – an attachment that wanted to attract to itself and take to its own lot all that was painful in the destiny of its object; that would, if it could, have absorbed and conducted away all storms and lightnings from an existence viewed with a passion of solicitude – then, just at that moment,the doors of my heart would shake, bolt and bar would yield, Reason would leap in vigorous and revengeful, snatch the full sheets, read, sneer, erase, tear up, re-write, fold, seal, direct, and send a terse, curt missive of a page. She did right. (*Villette*, Chapter Twenty-Three)

There is much to note here. There is the scale of the nominalisation that has turned human emotions into huge abstractions: Feeling, Reason, Love, Hope. Akin to this is the displacement of human feelings onto objects – 'an eager pen' – both procedures having the effect of pushing what is happening to Lucy away from her, and leading to a dramatisation of internal debate in almost allegorical form (the self as a theatre for the passions). Pronouns, too, behave in surprising ways ('nobody ever launches into Love unless *he* has seen...'); and are attracted into the orbit of abstractions that replace human beings as agents ('an attachment that wanted to attract to itself... all that was painful in the destiny of its object; that would... have absorbed and conducted away all storms and lightnings'). And then there is the tortuous syntax which could be analysed in detail but of which it seems enough to suggest here that the reader's struggle to follow it re-enacts Lucy's struggle to deny her own feelings for Dr John. Finally, the passage seems to erupt with all the violence implicit in that very denial ('snatch... sneer... erase ... ').

At the end of the day, readers still have choices to make, choices, which will be informed by values and beliefs. One way of looking at this passage (and at Lucy's whole story) would be in terms of a pathology. But against that reading we must set another: to argue that her dissociations and distrust of emotions are in fact strategies which enable her as a woman to survive and succeed in a patriarchal world. Under her circumstances emotional mutilation is the cost of taking control of your own life.

Even my account of this passage is a small-scale re-telling of the story. Listenings, too, are a sort of re-telling. On occasion, we may re-write or re-tell a first person narrative – for example in a supervision session, or with friends or colleagues – catching the urgency of what was said, but also trying to account for the gaps, following out the clues that lead to unspoken narratives. When we do so we are altering the point of view so as to achieve distancing effects, reformulating one telling within the scope of another. To re-tell a story within a new context has a re-framing effect, foregrounding unexpected aspects, and playing down others. Point of view and the control over point of view are a crucial component of an understanding of narrative. In first person narrative other points of view are implied: in third person narrative we commonly find that the point of view moves around.

One of the privileges attaching to the traditional novel is the convention of narrative omniscience, the fluidity of the boundaries which permit the narrator to know all that is going on that he or she judges pertinent to the story, and to enter into the consciousness and viewpoint of characters at will. On the face of it this influential and persistent convention seems rather an odd one, and it has certainly met with challenges in our own century, challenges which give rise to forms of writing to which we shall come back later. It seems likely that the convention of narrative omniscience has its roots in a continuum of interest in others extending from empathic curiosity at one end to prurience at the other, and taking in plain nosiness on the way. Human beings, as Nick Humphrey (1986) points out, spend their lives doing psychology, and our empathic powers have clearly served an evolutionary purpose. We need to know what it feels like to be other people, and we make exceedingly practical judgments on the basis of our projected knowledge. In fictions, the capacity of the narrative to enter into different points of view is always a selective ability: shooting from one camera angle has the negative implication that you are not shooting from another. While a character is viewed from the outside their inward being is concealed; alignment with the consciousness of one character means viewing others from outside.

Often, point of view is organised in a developmental sequence that mimes the journey from ignorance to knowledge, as a novelist (Hardy for example) will often begin with an outside view, reporting what you could have seen had you been present on Egdon Heath on such and such an afternoon, and the surmises you would have been able to make about the figures coming into your sight. At other times, the point of view moves out to focus on someone whom up till then we have only seen from a distance as an element in a scene. On such an occasion, the changed viewpoint brings about an alienation effect, whereby we see what has become familiar in a new perspective. Generally speaking, we find that the point of view of the novel moves between a narrative stance (looking at and reflecting upon the characters from without), and the consciousness of one or more of the characters. Someone whose viewpoint, motivation, hopes and anxieties is exposed to us may be adopted in fantasy as a temporary substitute self. The effect works even with someone who is represented from other points of view as unpleasant, oppressive, or cruel. The presentation can range from direct reportage of what a character thinks and sees to a mixture of authorial commentary with imagery and phrases which belong to the character whose mindstyle we are being urged to adopt. Consciousness can be indicated by little give-aways:

> Alan was waiting in the Lyceum café for his sister Madge. He hadn't seen her for fifteen years and she was already three-quarters of an hour late. The waitress had asked him twice if he cared to order anything. He said he would just hold on if it was all the same to her.... [He] felt in the pocket of his black overcoat, to make sure that the envelope containing Mother's engagement ring was still safe. Madge had never liked jewellery. His wife Joan had told him he must ask Madge to foot the bill for having it insured all these months. It was only fair. He'd paid for the flowers and the notice in the newspaper. Madge hadn't even bothered to turn up at the funeral. (Beryl Bainbridge, *A Quiet Life*, Chapter 0)

Here what looks at first like straight narration is mixed in with indicators of point of view. So 'already... late', 'only fair', 'hadn't even bothered' represent not an impartial statement of the case, but Alan (and his wife's) account of events. We may imagine them enclosed in inverted commas as the things they would say to one another.

Part of the function of the novel has traditionally been to move between viewpoints in such a way as to call upon the reader to imagine things from new angles, asking us to enter in to consciousnesses that feel at first unsympathetic and foreign. A theory of sympathy has long been around in the practices of writing and reading novels. D.H. Lawrence was speaking for an established tradition when he wrote:

> After all, one may hear the most private affairs of other people, but only in a spirit of respect for the struggling, battered thing which any human soul is, and in a spirit of fine, discriminative sympathy... It is the way our sympathy flows and recoils that really determines our lives. And here lies the vast importance of the novel, properly handled. It can inform and lead into new places the flow of our sympathetic consciousness, and it can lead our sympathy away in recoil from things gone dead. (*Lady Chatterley's Lover*, Chapter Nine)

Ironically, in view of what I said above, this is put in the mouth of the narrator. However, it concurs with a number of things Lawrence says in his own person elsewhere. Such a notion of sympathy may reinforce people's sense of literature as a gallery of characters. I take it that part of the unconscious appeal of storytelling (and perhaps of the figure of the narrator who knows all) is the hope that our own tribulations and sufferings, all the daily misunderstandings, unfairnesses and injustices, will find someone to listen with loving and undistracted attention. It is a fantasy we can indulge in the reading of a those novels which hold their characters in something akin to an idealised parental embrace. There is, I think, an affinity between the traditional narrator and the counsellor. One of the things people are looking for in counselling may be something very similar to the figure of the traditional narrator: a wise presence, or witness who listens to and can comprehend all the competing sub-narratives that go to the make up of your larger story.

Yet the novel which is organised around wisdom creates its own hierarchies and exclusions. Before leaving the subject of point of view and the simulation of character, I want to point out the existence of forms of narrative which have themselves abandoned the control and mobility of viewpoint exercised by the omniscient narrator. We may identify various factors at work in this shift, all of them highly relevant to the narrative paradigms available in the everyday. They include a feeling that traditional third person narration was not in fact realistic enough, and that you must find ways of telling that do justice to the precise specificities of human experience. More fundamentally, they represent scepticism about the potential of narrative itself, a doubt whether an objective vision that would gather up everything and see people's lives whole was possible or even desirable. There has thus been a twentieth-century trend towards narratives that experiment with multiple versions, where each version is trapped inside the simulated consciousness of a particular character. The task of the reader in novels like William Faulkner's *As I Lay Dying*, and *The Sound and the Fury*, or Milan Kundera's *The Joke* is one of sifting the different versions of the story that different characters tell, and seeing where they mesh and where they conflict. To that extent such a realism exactly parallels our attempts to weigh what people say to us in real life. There we have no recourse to an authoritative narrator who sees and knows all, and arbitrates between conflicting claims to the truth. Novels which mime this procedure are informed by a more general scepticism within western culture about the possibility of attaining the truth, or about the presence of a final arbitrator.

This impulse towards greater fidelity to the feel and texture of human experience also feeds into that mode which appeared in the early years of the century and to which people give the name of 'interior monologue' or 'stream of consciousness', a mode of writing associated with the work of authors such as Virginia Woolf, Dorothy Richardson, and James Joyce.

> If it were fine they should go for a picnic. Everything seemed possible. Everything seemed right. Just now (but this cannot last, she thought, dissociating herself from the moment while they were all talking about boots) just now she had reached security; she hovered like a hawk suspended; like a flag floated in an element of joy which filled every nerve of her body fully and sweetly, not noisily, solemnly rather, for it arose, she thought, looking at them all eating there, from husband and children and

friends; all of which rising in this profound stillness (she was helping William Bankes to one very small piece more and peered into the depths of the earthenware pot) seemed now for no special reason to stay there like a smoke, like a fume rising upwards holding them safe together. Nothing need be said; nothing could be said. There it was, all round them. It partook, she felt, carefully helping Mr Bankes to a specially tender piece, of eternity; as she had already felt about something different once before that afternoon: there is a coherence in things, a stability; something, she meant, is immune from change, and shines out (she glanced at the window with its ripple of reflected lights) in the face of the flowing, the fleeting, the spectral, like a ruby; so that again tonight she had the feeling she had had once today already,of peace, of rest. (Virginia Woolf, *To the Lighthouse*, 'The Window', Chapter Seventeen)

This passage by Virginia Woolf enacts Mrs Ramsay's thoughts as she presides over the dinner for family and guests. It differs from traditional reported thought in being less coherent, less logical, and in setting out to catch the way one thought will interrupt another, the simultaneity of act and reverie, the way in which a mood will seize you and lend its colour to what you see around. At the same time, the passage clearly works within conventions to do with the use of elaborate syntax and with what kinds of thought get represented. That even interior monologue needs to inhabit conventions may be more apparent if we take a contrasting excerpt from another family meal:

Bringing things from there to here. Moving from one position to the one that comes next. A sprinkle of magic dust and a boisterous abracadabra, the puff of smoke and Pat materialising back in his own kitchen in front of the fire. He should have gone straight home after the match. He just shouldni have come here. How come he came? He shouldni have fucking came. It was stupid. Guilt probably. His first visit in three weeks – nearer a month in fact. Who cares. No point in worrying over it.

The fish was a dead animal. It had lain there on the plate open for inspection, eager to impress s/he who is about to partake. Just please devour me. I'm as good as the next thing you'll catch. Whatever you do dont not do it, dont not devour me, I'm a good wee fish. Courageous and heroic. Its body sliced open for examination by the education authority. Give it a tick. A plus. Five out of ten. Fine for a Glasgow table but dont send it south to the posher restaurants of England.

Gibberish. Outpourings. People see facial expressions of silence, not seeing, not

How is it all contained? The heads craned over the plates, the three people eating, this man and woman and man, while within the limits of each an intense caterwaul. We are alone! We are isolate beings! The good Lord alone

Fucking bastards. (James Kelman, *A Disaffection*, p.114)

This passage seeks to capture the way thoughts, associations, quotations flicker across the consciousness by using repetition, puns, and a lot of short sentences.

Traditional syntax and punctuation is strained to catch some one in a state of manic excitement – near hysteria even – talking to themselves (interior monologue is clearly a misnomer). Its system of notation is nevertheless inevitably dependent on the nature of writing. Writing is linear and finds it difficult to represent simultaneity; such a discourse not only has to represent in words fragmentary and half-formed thoughts but even sensations. It will exercise editing of its own over what reaches the page, and manage entrances and exits. Nevertheless, the struggle to find a notation for the sensation of serial consciousness has enriched our narrative repertoire, even while reminding us that the pursuit of realism has ever to be carried on within conventions and rhetorical devices. We ought also to note that in attracting all the attention to interiority this inward turn (which parallels a widespread psychologisation of thought) may distract attention from the various outer forces shaping people's lives.

In the section on narrative I pointed out that the provision of endings was a prime source of narrative satisfaction. There are many ways of constructing an ending, and probably the vast majority of written fictions move towards a closure that is not simply the consequence of running out of space. A sequence of events comes to an end, a mystery is solved, two characters who have been kept apart for most of the narrative find each other. Critics sometimes contrast the plot of resolution with the plot of revelation. But whether based upon revelation of something hidden till then, or resolution of plot suspense, conventions of closure become so familiar that we notice them only when we come across a narrative which refuses to end in an expectable way. Many twentieth-century writers have experimented with other kinds of ending, leaving the reader with an enigma, a deciphering job: a nagging doubt as to what it all means. The final scene may be an act of witnessing, as when at the end of *To the Lighthouse* (Virginia Woolf), Lily Briscoe sees the Ramsay party arrive on the island, and is suddenly moved to complete her picture. We may leave the protagonist alone like Paul at the end of *Sons and Lovers* (D.H. Lawrence), contemplating the vastness of the universe. There is a contrast between ending with an enigmatic act of witnessing or contemplation, and ending with the triumphant wrapping up of the events of the plot, and as readers our sense of completion will be affected accordingly. Generally, the closer to the interior a novel has been (or the more insistently first person) the less likely it is to close with a plotted conclusion, and the more likely to offer an event which we are invited to understand as symbolic but not 'the end'. Being left with the image of the protagonist running away from the police (*A Disaffection*, James Kelman), or with a friend's ring at the door (*The Member of the Wedding*, Carson McCullers) may dissatisfy in one way, but in another heightens the sense of presence, by suggesting a continuing life outside the pages of the story. It also leaves the reader firmly in that interpretative role which so much twentieth-century fiction invites the reader to share with the narrator. With an eye to

counselling, and aware of the pun, we might say that such fictions offer us a final
(if ambiguous) disclosure.

SUGGESTIONS FOR FURTHER READING

Erich Auerbach (trans. Willard Trask) (1953) *Mimesis: the Representation of Reality in
Western Literature*, Princeton UP.

Roland Barthes (trans. Richard Miller) (1975) *S/Z*. London: Jonathan Cape.

Seymour Chatman (1978) *Story and Discourse: Narrative Structure in Fiction and Film*.
Ithaca, NY: Cornell UP.

Steven Cohan and Linda Shires (1988) *Telling Stories: a Theoretical Analysis of Narrative
Fiction*. London: Routledge.

Kathryn Hume (1984) *Fantasy and Mimesis: Responses to Reality in Western Literature*.
London: Methuen.

Rosemary Jackson (1981) *Fantasy: the Literature of Subversion*. London: Methuen.

David Lodge (1977) *The Modes of Modern Writing*. London: Arnold.

Janice A. Radway (1987) *Reading the Romance: Women, Patriarchy, and Popular Literature*.
London: Verso.

Elaine Showalter (1977) *A Literature of Their Own: British Women Novelists from Brontë to
Lessing*. London: Virago.

CHAPTER SEVEN

Talking Through a Novel
The Awakening

I think that the best way to follow through and develop the argument of the last chapter will be to take as an example a more prolonged reading of a specific text. I propose to 'talk through' Kate Chopin's short novel *The Awakening*. You may wish, with the text in front of you, to use this chapter as a guide in your exploration (page references are to the Women's Press edition). It can, of course, be no more than a guide, an additional (and I hope helpful) partner in the conversation between reader and text. I have chosen *The Awakening* both for its own sake, and as an example of the novel at work: I hope that much of what I have to say about it will be relevant to the reading of any fiction, although at the same time we should acknowledge the specificity of this particular text.

A brief introduction goes like this. Kate Chopin (1850–1904), although born in St Louis, Missouri, lived for her married life in New Orleans. After her husband's death in 1882, she began to write, producing short stories, poems, essays, and novels, of which *The Awakening* (which was the subject of public outrage and condemnation after it was published in 1899) was the last. In the 1970s and 1980s and under the influence of feminism the novel has become widely read – certainly in this country – as part of the construction of an alternative and emancipatory literary canon: a novel of liberation, despite the death of its heroine.

It follows from all I have been saying that there are modalities of reading just as there are modalities of text. Even within the reading of the same text and within the same few minutes the skilled reader will be likely to move between one mode of reading and another, varying the focus, speed, and nature of attention. The fact that I shall move through this text picking out certain items and generalising about their significance within the larger scheme of the book does not imply that the only way to read is to plod laboriously forward, levering problems out of the pages and cross-questioning them. Nor does it mean that the only way of reading a literary text is with a kind of alert wariness, an unblinking determination not to be fooled. But I hope that paying attention to details and structures on some occasions has the effect of heightening awareness at others. The aim is not a bravura decoding of an inert novel, but an activity of reading which calls into being energies of attention and noticing. Novels provide us with simulated networks of relationships and communication, and much of the point of this book would be lost if the reader went away believing that critical reading could be written off as a matter of stripping books down with an all-purpose toolkit. The role of reader, like that of counsellor, requires the availability of a repertoire of concepts and mental models. But in both roles, concepts and models can be worn as an armour against the perils of encounter. This book does not intend to advocate such an evasion. Analytical understanding should complement sensitivity, not replace it. At the same time, it is a piece of misplaced romanticism to suppose that sensitivity cannot be developed.

STARTING OFF

The first chapter sets a scene (the Lebruns' holiday cottages outside New Orleans, frequented by 'exclusive visitors from the *Quartier Français*') and introduces us to the Pontelliers. It starts, however, with Mr. Pontellier. As the novel is written in the third person, we know that point of view is likely to be mobile, and our first glimpse of Mrs Pontellier is located within her husband's gaze. She is seen as an object, identified with her white sunshade ('He fixed his gaze upon a white sunshade that was advancing at snail's pace from the beach.' White is of course – presumably because any stain shows up on it – conventionally a sign of purity). While the gaze is his, we are also introduced to a narrative voice, a 'voice over' which says of him that he looked at his wife 'as one looks at a valuable piece of personal property which has suffered some damage' (p.7). This narrator clearly has views on the Pontelliers' relationship, and is also capable of dropping in what appears to be reportage to which readers are left to attach significance – like the father leaving for the club promising to bring back bonbons and peanuts. In fact, we do not subsequently hear much about Mr Pontellier's point of view, and the novel tends to move between those of the narrator and of Edna.

A first chapter will also introduce items about whose significance we may be left wondering. This one offers us the sea, the beach, and the related topic of bathing, which taken together may compose what Roland Barthes would call a 'seme', a unit of meaning. As we pick up the references to this group of signifiers, they start to form a code, a narrative thread which entwines itself with other narrative threads to generate what we experience as the novel. As we become aware of repetitions and juxtapositions we are becoming aware of what we might call the inner story within the outer story, although at first we cannot know behind which items inner significance lurks. Items may, be so to speak, hanging loose, leaving us wondering about their possible significance. Is the green and yellow parrot an item in a chain, or a circumstantial detail? There is nothing here to help us be sure: while parrots are noted for saying things without knowing what they are saying, this one is an enigma, and enigmas await resolution (we might provisionally note, though, that it is a living being, kept for ornamental reasons in a cage). Other subjects placed before us are marriage (the emphasis on the positional titles Mr and Mrs, the foregrounding of the rings – to be picked up later in the scene where Edna throws her ring on the floor) and Robert Lebrun as a 'third party'. Readers are invited into a process of hypothesis and filling out indeterminate blanks with significance which will then have to be tested against what actually happens. Which is to say that reading (like listening) is a perpetual process of forming, testing, and rejecting hypothesis about where the story is going, and the significance of the items brought to your attention.

FORM AND STRUCTURE

As we read *The Awakening*, we shall be picking out matters of form as well as meaning, and indeed the distinction is not one that can be sustained for long. In governing and shaping the reading process, form plays a major part in organising the meanings we can assign to a text. Form, says Kenneth Burke, is 'the creation of an appetite in the mind of an auditor, and the adequate satisfying of that appetite'. Form, that is to say, does not exist outside the rhetorical relation. It is evident, for example, that *The Awakening* is divided into very short chapters of but a few pages, even occasionally a single page each. Once we have noted this, and the rapid succession of episodes to which it gives rise, we are in a position to be on the alert for the way in which short chapters affect our reading experience. Thus I note that they make possible rapid shifts of point of view, tone, and scene; also that through the emphatic weight that falls on endings, they create between them what becomes a narrative motif: ending a chapter with an understatement, an apparently innocuous detail, which contains within it a germ to be developed.

> He kissed them and promised to bring them back bonbons and peanuts.
>
> ... he amused himself with the little Pontellier children, who were very fond of him.
>
> Mrs. Pontellier was forced to admit that she knew of [no husband] better.
>
> Mrs. Pontellier gave over being astonished, and concluded that wonders would never cease.

Any novel models the kind of attention which reading it will require; here, the short chapters, the narrative understatement, and the presence of a cast of characters and scenes which is large relative to the length of the novel passes a lot of the work of attention and holding possibilities together to the reader. A chapter ending might almost be visualised as a row of dots inviting the reader to supply more meaning than the final sentences apparently warrant.

Chapter endings are, however, only one among a multitude of signs that a reader learns to pick up as he or she gets familiar with a text. There is a real sense in which getting to know a text is to learn its language, to become accustomed to its style, its mannerisms, the kind of thing it talks about, where it is likely to put emphases. Much of this work of getting attuned we do intuitively. Literary criticism holds that to have the process out in the open and inspect it sometimes has a beneficial effect on subsequent reading. It is a bit like studying the videotape of a group session: you notice more next time. Because the intention is to encourage readers to develop their own reading, this commentary will not run to the same detail throughout, but will home in on some things and leave others to you.

Before picking up some issues from the opening, I would like to explore a bit further some thoughts on this novel's mode of operation. Short chapters, we have seen, are one feature of the text's shaping dialogue with the reader. To this we might add that the characteristic matrix within which meaning is produced is narrative punctuated by dialogue, the narrative itself composed variously of passages of description of scenes and places, a chronicle of events, and reports on the thought processes of the characters. At times one modality predominates over others: Chapter Eleven, for example, foregrounds dialogue, in providing a lucid account of the sexual games people play. Much of the process of the novel seems to be guided by concern with how the unspoken and unacknowledged can enter into the public domain, a topos of disclosure. Thus on Robert's departure 'Edna bit her handkerchief convulsively, striving to hold back and to hide, even from herself as she would have hidden from another, the emotion that was troubling – tearing her' (p.75). A few pages later the narrator comments:

> She had all her life long been accustomed to harbor thoughts and emotions which never voiced themselves. They had never taken the form of struggles. They belonged to her and were her own, and she entertained the conviction that she had a right to them and they concerned no one but herself. (p.79)

Novels have made it one of their aims to find a sharable language for that which was unspoken and hidden, but we should not suppose that that makes the telling any easier. The struggle to find words is a formal struggle, and we should not be surprised to discover that the form of the novel, the frame in which the telling is cast, reflects the problems of setting words upon emotions that have been hidden and unacknowledged – for which there is, as yet, no communal language.

In *The Awakening* the topos of bringing out into the open (which is itself 'the awakening', since new emotions demand new actions) shapes the textual procedure. As Frank Kermode points out, fictions convert mere succession (the chronology of the day to day) into significance (*Sense of an Ending*, part 2), and it seems to me that the theme of awakening is apparent in the novel's considerable vagueness about time. For while it is true that the novel does follow a linear

Murrell Library
Missouri Valley College
Marshall, Missouri 65340

chronology, and that it is possible to work out the time framework from the information given, the inner time links which connect one chapter with another are characteristically either unstated or take the form of 'one morning', 'that summer afternoon', 'that summer she began to loosen a little the mantle of reserve', 'a few weeks later', 'one evening' and so on. The holes in time may also be the gaps where the reader's own unconscious involvement can twist itself into the trellis of the fiction. This novel works as a succession of episodes whose significance is only partially spelled out: one effect of this is that while we await disclosure, and look out for explanations of why episodes have been brought to our attention, the novel does not work by a build up of suspense such as we might find in a highly-plotted novel (like a thriller, for instance). The playing down of time as chronology or imposed framework also has the effect of heightening the prominence of episodes in providing thematic cohesion. Brightly lit moments emerge out of the chronological haze: the plot advances not so much along the lines of a chronicle which is explicit about time and about causation, but through a sequence of episodes where some of the text's prime signifiers gather. An example of this is the linked sequence of Chapters Nine to Fourteen, where Mlle. Reisz's recital leads to the moonlit swim, to Edna's sexual withdrawal from her husband, to the boat trip to Grande Terre.

At a psychological level we might say that this vagueness enacts the dreamy state of Edna Pontellier, propelled along by forces she does not understand. Indeed sleep and dreams feature repeatedly as they must in this awakening. We might even draw the conclusion that significant change is likely to take place in a haze, the self on such occasions being swept along by forces of which it has little understanding and less control. At a textual level we further observe that this is a text where events are organised by interrelated symbolic episodes rather than by the explicit causational logic of one event leading to another. *The Awakening* does not work by continuously rising drama, and it may well be that this more low key procedure of slow arousal represents an attempt to subvert the climactic management of tension of the traditional (masculine) novel. To the subject of symbolism and organising symbols we shall return when we have taken account of other features that the early stages of the novel place before us.

POINTS OF VIEW

It appears that part of the procedure of this novel is to offer a series of short scenes, or vignettes whose presence and role in the forward movement of the narrative is not conclusively explained by a narrative voice-over. Nevertheless, the persona of the narrator evidently does hold views on things, as we see in the sample of the Pontelliers' married life that occurs in Chapter Three; we are evidently to become accustomed to a narrative which supplies information and evaluations at some times and withholds it at others (thus of Edna's marriage to Léonce Pontellier: 'She fancied there was a sympathy of thought and taste between them, in which fancy she was mistaken.' p.32). We readers have to learn to pick up the hints and clues the text offers. Look for a moment at the first page of Chapter Three. Mr Pontellier comes back in high good humour from the club to find that his wife is virtually asleep.

> He thought it very discouraging that his wife who was the sole object of his existence, evinced so little interest in things that concerned him, and valued so little his conversation.

We are faced with a choice: this little paragraph could be from Mr Pontellier's point of view, reported without comment by the narrator. It could be 'indirect speech', reporting what he said to his wife in a half-jokey, complaining way. My sense of it is that the next paragraph holds the clue:

> Mr. Pontellier had forgotten the bonbons and peanuts for the boys. Notwithstanding he loved them very much, and went into the adjoining room where they slept to take a look at them and make sure they were resting comfortably. The result of his investigation was far from satisfactory.

We are, I think, in the presence of a powerful irony, an irony which precludes sympathy with Mr Pontellier. Why do I think this? Partly because from what I know of the narrator I cannot believe that she takes Mr Pontellier at his own valuation; partly on stylistic grounds: 'evinced... valued so little', 'notwithstanding', 'far from satisfactory' seem to belong to a pompous register attributed to him. This conviction is heightened when we realise that he is merely fault-finding about Raoul's health and using the child to advance his own view of the protectiveness that motherliness should entail. There's a narrative hint as well in the recurrence of the gift item, bonbons coding a fatherly attitude that translates caring for people into giving (or at least promising) expensive and capricious treats (the chapter ends with another gift, the box of expensive tit-bits – which Mrs Pontellier is quite used to receiving). Our interpretation of the Pontelliers and the relationship between them is not the result of direct narrative intervention alone. There are ways of commenting on Mr Pontellier's habits and assumptions without overt judgment. It is at least possible that readers feel more involved in judgments which they have played a part in forming themselves. Further, they are likely to react against judgements where they feel themselves the hapless subjects of narrative preaching. If Chapter Three opens our eyes to the Pontelliers' marriage, it also paves the way to a discussion of motherliness and fatherliness which is continued in the next chapter.

Here, and throughout the rest of the novel, the motherly motif is largely organised around the figure of Madame Ratignolle ('Think of the children...' is her last and horrendously effective line to her friend) to whom we are introduced in a flurry of 'mother' compounds – 'mother-tots', 'mother woman'. We may note that such linguistic deviations – here the invention of compound words – have an alienation effect upon their subject matter, on this occasion re-framing as

TALKING THROUGH A NOVEL 101

grotesque the identification of womanliness with motherliness. As with Mr Pontellier's gaze down the beach we are confronted with the masculinist assumptions of point of view, and it appears to me that the whole of *The Awakening* operates a quiet subversion of the presumption of masculinity in the beholder. The give-away line in Chapter Four follows the paragraph that proclaims of the 'mother-women'

> They were women who idolized their children, worshipped their husbands, and esteemed it a holy privilege to efface themselves as individuals and grow wings as ministering angels... Many of them were delicious in the role...

The 'delicious' (like the bonbons? – food as metaphor pervades the text) clearly belongs, like the 'one would not have wanted' which follows, not with the narrator but with an interwoven masculine viewpoint. Madame Ratignolle is herself largely the creation of this viewpoint, a creature of flamboyant and externally described charms, and her persistence in mother role throughout the novel provides us with grounds for reflecting upon role in narrative.

ROLES AND RELATIONS

In a previous chapter I proposed that 'characters' in fiction should be seen as roles in perpetual interplay with each other, and as figures 'carrying' values and attributes important within the narrative. There was, I suggested, an illuminating analogy between the novel text and the group. I return to the topic here in an attempt to document the procedure in action. I want to get at two, related, things. One is that the narrative repertoire of 'character' itself varies, from text to text, and also within texts. There is a continuum: at one end the characters of folk story, romance, or allegory who are very plainly 'one-dimensional, bearers of the needs of the plot, or moral 'types'. At the other the characters who turn up in many nineteenth and twentieth century novels, realised with a high degree of psychological verisimilitude. In this novel, for example, we have a range extending from Edna Pontellier herself through to the anonymous pair of lovers who turn up on crucial occasions, ghosting, as it were, the main lovers. But the second and related thing is that it is possible both to fulfil the readerly desire to fill out the characters of fiction psychologically, and to recognise the possibility of seeing them as figures or types. I want to distinguish between 'figure' and 'type': figure to me implies the character's role in the drama which may well involve change; type the character as a set of more or less static traits – the two plainly overlap.

The point of all this is that 'characters' operate within – may even derive from – the dynamic of the narrative. They are mutually related roles, not self-contained entities. One way of thinking this in psychodynamic terms is to scan 'characters' as a set of interrelated traits, or sub-selves where each has one or two attributes highly developed. So reading fiction may involve us in the recognition of split off or dissociated bits, aspects of the self which turn into caricature in isolation.

On this showing, different novels present us with opportunities to recognise potential dissociated fragments: the alienated life of undeveloped emotions and capacities, our potential androgyny, or our wistful or revengeful child-selves – all manner of latencies and potentials which for diverse cultural and individual reasons we have never developed. We both recognise these and witness their integration in a larger drama. Within this drama characters change and develop. Textual figures are thus analogous at the social level to the roles we find ourselves playing, and at the level of the self to the fragmented parts of our own internal drama. John Rowan (1990), for example, has recognised that the 'whole area of the work of the novelist is of course very much open to examination from the point of view of subpersonalities' (p.38 and compare Chapter Eight). A lot of his argument is relevant to what I am saying here, although I would prefer to emphasise the work that the text calls on the reader to do rather than the presence of hypothetical subpersonalities of the author. It is as easy to stereotype aspects of ourselves as it is to stereotype others, and fiction offers us a space in which to mobilise change by loosening the distorting power of such sterotypes.

A moment ago I distinguished between figures and types. Following this distinction, Mme Ratignolle may be a type of motherhood as sexually winning, but a figure in this particular text where she operates in opposition and contrast to other models of being a woman. In asserting that characters may be seen as figures I am not trying to deny either the readerly need for character, or fiction's potential for simulating highly complex persons. Rather, I am suggesting the need for a stereoscopic vision capable of acknowledging that even psychologically plausible characters also carry aspects of the narrative as a whole, and that in doing so they enact for us readers split off latencies of the self. Far from novels or plays resulting from the author bringing some characters together and seeing what happens, the characters (even at their most individually convincing) are a function of the needs of the narrative. Let us take the example of Mlle Reisz.

> She was a disagreeable little woman, no longer young, who had quarreled with almost everyone, owing to a temper which was self-assertive and a disposition to trample upon the rights of others... She was a homely woman, with a small weazened face and body and eyes that glowed. She had absolutely no taste in dress, and wore a batch of rusty black lace with a bunch of artificial violets pinned to the side of her hair. (p.43)

The artificial violets become her call sign. The description and the *artificiality* of the violets seem to code that within the anonymous masculine viewpoint she is no longer sexual game. We have I think to discriminate between the narrative voice and whoever it is who views Mlle Reisz in this fashion. 'She had absolutely no taste in dress' appears to be the judgement of the fashionable community, and one might generalise to suppose that the other objections are too. Indeed within the narrative argument which is unfolding, self-assertiveness and a willingness to trample on the rights of others compare positively with the docile feminine submissiveness elsewhere. Mlle Reisz is the name of a woman who refuses to fit in (she has some of the attributes of the witch). To that extent she stands for the possibility of autonomy and living your own life, a role model which she offers throughout the unfolding of her relations with Edna Pontellier. But she has another figural significance as well. She is a musician.

We do not need wholeheartedly to embrace the notion current a few years ago that works of art were totally self-referential, to be impressed by the enormous number of references to art and artists that occur in fictions. Art in one form or another may in the context of verbal fiction stand for the art in hand; painters and musicians frequently provide ways of working at problems concerning writing. But art and music also sometimes turn up in novels as a kind of test of authenticity, a code which discriminates between those who genuinely understand and are moved by them, and those who only pretend to, and thus between those whom the novel values and those whom it does not. So it is that in Chapter Nine Edna is so moved by Mlle Reisz's playing that she cannot speak her reply to the question how she has liked the music. 'You are the only one worth playing for. Those others? Bah!' replies the pianist who leaves to a chorus of inauthenticity, signalled by the narrator's tongue-in-cheek comment that

> ... she was mistaken about 'those others'. Her playing had aroused a fever of enthusiasm. 'What passion!' 'What an artist' 'I have always said no one could play Chopin like Mademoiselle Reisz!' 'That last prelude! Bon Dieu! It shakes a man'. (p.45)

The point is not only that the music provides a test for who is genuine and who is not. It is that since music (which may indeed parallel the work of another Chopin – novelists and poets are not above puns on their own names) is seen as a means of expression, and playing a demonstration of the possibility of being in touch with your deepest emotions, those who treat it as mere entertainment and pretext for prattle are committing the nearest thing in the novel to sacrilege. In the contrary condition, Mrs Pontellier is ready, perhaps for the first time, 'to take an impress of the abiding truth'. Mlle Reisz and her piano playing play a crucial part in her quest for freedom. She provides an alternative model of being a woman to that provided by Mme Ratignolle, good natured as she is. And music can perhaps here provide a code for the praxis of the female novelist, finding a voice in which to speak of tyranny, freedom, and desire. By contrast, Edna's own effort to take up painting is clearly too bound by class limitations to lead her anywhere.

I am not seeking to provide a complete inventory of the textual roles played by the characters of *The Awakening*, but I would like to allude to two more, as having perhaps a more general significance. Just as the novel provides possible roles for women, it also offers masculine roles. Thus (and even leaving aside the principal characters) Alcée Arobin, represents the rake, the sexually predatory male. He serves the function of arousing Edna to her own sexuality, but his opportunism and shallowness offer her nothing else. And the Doctor is a type who turns up repeatedly in fiction, and indeed (strikingly for our purposes) in Ibsen's contemporary plays about women's attempts to re-route their lives: the doctor as wise man, an elder male with the capacity to listen, to befriend and to offer advice. 'He knew his fellow creatures better than most men, knew that inner life which so seldom unfolds itself to unanointed eyes' (p.118). It is interesting in the context of this book that figures of counsellors recur in fiction – fiction indeed commonly provides a critique of the limitations of the role. Here Doctor Mandelet with his kindly if blinkered vision is no answer. Edna cannot in the end turn to him for help since what she needs lies beyond anything that it is on his power to advise. The novelist, who herself attends to the inner lives of persons, is understandably fascinated by those who listen, and at the same time intrigued and horrified by the risks attaching to giving advice.

SYMBOLS AND SIGNIFIERS

The piano and music, we have seen, provide us with an example of a topos, a signifier whose recurrence in the text exceeds the demands of circumstantial detail, and becomes thematic. As we have observed in previous chapters, a metaphor of this order offers a surplus of meaning; while we can translate it into other terms (e.g. music in this novel 'stands for' the expression of emotion), we find a signifying energy that goes beyond such direct translation. Such items seem to constitute what we know as 'symbols', and it seems to me that the disclosures of *The Awakening* are organised around certain powerful symbols, of which the most prominent (though certainly not the only one) is the sea. Much of the novel is set at the sea side, and major episodes concern crossing the sea to Grande Terre, and Edna's learning to swim. In the end she dies by swimming beyond her strength out into the Gulf of Mexico. But it is not simply the repetition of references to the sea, swimming, boats, and so on which alert our attention to this symbolic field. The narrator also steps in to direct our attention to the matter. If you look at the opening of Chapter Six, you will see that the narrative voice makes a series of observations. Edna, it says, is impelled by two contradictory impulses: she 'was beginning to realize her position in the universe as a human being'. The passage that follows, having evoked the holy ghost, then refers to the opening of the creation passage of the Book of Genesis. Edna is emerging from the formless just as the creation emerged (though admittedly under the tutelage of a male God).

Here we are confronted with the profound ambiguity of the ancient symbol of the sea. It is without form and void, the water on which the spirit moved. But it is also 'seductive... inviting the soul to wander for a spell in abysses of solitude, to lose itself in mazes of inward contemplation'. 'The touch of the sea is sensuous, enfolding the body in its soft, close embrace.' Presumably the sea is traditionally associated with passion (and how flat it seems to put it like that) precisely because it offers an image of vastness and dissolution, a return to what Freud spoke of as the 'oceanic feeling'. That dissolution is at once the merging of individuality in something greater, and death. It may be that the most profound symbols always exhibit a deep ambivalence, and that people turn to them because they hold together potentials for meaning that exceed local operational demands. At all events, the sea in *The Awakening* as much as in *Tristan und Isolde* is simultaneously the element through which it is possible to voyage to a new life (a form of mobility in a life characterised by stasis), and the formless, queasy medium which both threatens and promises dissolution and return to nothingness. Here, learning to swim, and exposure to the sea's 'sensuous embrace' plainly prefigure Edna's entry into an aroused sexuality. She suddenly succeeds in learning to swim on the moonlit night after Mlle Reisz's recital (Chapter Ten):

> She turned her face to seaward to gather in an impression of space and solitude, which the vast expanse of water, meeting and melting with the moonlit sky, conveyed to her excited fancy. As she swam she seemed to be reaching out for the unlimited in which to lose herself. (p.48)

This moment is then picked up in the final scene when Edna sheds her clothes and steps into the sea for the last time, a moment where like a phrase in music, the phrase from Chapter Six returns: 'The touch of the sea is sensuous, enfolding the body in its soft, close embrace'.

The sea, I have suggested, is this book's central symbol. We should not visualise such a symbol as standing by itself, but as producing meaning within a signifying structure. Significance is generated by contrast. The sea, vast, soothing and elemental, contrasts with the pettiness of the organisation of life on the margins of the land: such oppositions persist throughout the text. In tabular form, some of these oppositions would look like this:

mobility	stasis
sea	land
activity	passivity
awakening	dreaming
music	superficial painting
authentic speech	inauthentic speech

In these terms the seaside realm of pampered holiday (which supersedes in many ways the ancient, alternative rural location of 'pastoral') is paradoxically the place not of finding yourself, but a cage where women and children are kept while the men enjoy the freedom that work gives them. Edna's journey in this novel consists in the effort to move from one of the zones defined in this table to the other, a movement attended for historical reasons by disaster.

Before we move on I would like to notice one more symbolic cluster. Food and eating pervade the novel, both the meals at Mme Lebrun's, and the sugary delicacies which code the comfortable (and dependent) life lived in this perpetual holiday while the men are at work. The food code seems to lead like a trail to that episode in Chapter Thirty where Edna holds a dinner for a group of ill-assorted guests before moving to her new house. The event leads to a further development of her sexual relationship with Arobin. In narrative terms, the occasion serves the function of reversal (Edna is taking command of food giving, and potentially of her own space; may even be about to throw of the bonds of infantilising wealth), but it is a reversal which does not actually lead, as it would in comedy, to a new situation. The symbolism of eating together, of a party, calls for further decoding, especially since the narrator does not step in to explain. In attempting to unpick the inner story I am struck by overlaid connotations. The meal (like Mrs Ramsay's meal in *To the Lighthouse*) bespeaks a servanted world, and the wealth on which the lives of these characters is based. To that extent it seems to represent conspicuous consumption. But we do not exhaust the symbol at that point. There is, it seems to me, an erotic connotation often attached (at least by men) to eating and drinking – the young mothers, we remember, looked 'delicious'; while of Cleopatra it is said 'other women cloy/ The appetites they feed, but she makes hungry/ Where most she satisfies'. At another level still, a failed ceremony, an attempt at a celebratory event that does not come off, that ends in disillusionment or disaster, is a topos repeated again and again in literature. In this particular context it seems to speak of all the failures of social life to yield satisfactory forms. In this context this must include in particular the failed ceremony of marriage into which Edna has walked with eyes half-closed.

The repetition of such persistent signifiers as the sea, swimming, eating, or festivity is closely related to what we know as themes or thematic material. *The Awakening*, like any other fiction, is organised around certain themes, themes which have been the subject of exploration elsewhere. Adultery is one such theme in Kate Chopin's novel. One source of the interest which fiction has taken in this subject may well have to do, as Tony Tanner suggests, with its capacity to act as a metaphor for all kinds of transgression against social rules, and for a radicalism that refuses to acknowledge or be bound by manufactured constraints. Chopin seems to be reclaiming the adultery motif for women and women's fiction. For *The Awakening's* great predecessors which took this theme were written by men about women. I'm thinking of novels often cited as among the first rank in European literature, novels like Flaubert's *Madame Bovary*, Tolstoy's *Anna Karenin*, or Fontane's *Effi Briest*. Different though these are, in each of them a woman, trapped in an intolerable or boring marriage tries to find a way out through an adulterous relationship. Like Edna Pontellier, they end up dead. But before condemning the novel as an agent of social control, or as a symbolic and barbarous vengeance carried out by outraged men upon female desire, we need to touch for a moment on the ambivalent nature of cultural works.

In essence, what I want to say is this. We hope for too much if we want cultural works to stand pure and unfettered on the side of progress or enlightenment, a mountain range of soaring peaks of wisdom. A novel purged of all the limitations of its time is a chimera, a fantasy. Works of art are capable of demonstrating at one and the same time potentialities which are liberating, and others which are reactionary and enclosing. The point is not so much that Flaubert and Tolstoy (or Kate Chopin, Ibsen or Hardy) did not come up with a better solution for their heroines, but that they tried at all, testing out and reinforcing through their novels subtle social changes through which women's submissive role in a patriarchal world was slowly coming to be seen as problematic and questionable. Like these predecessors, Kate Chopin was enquiring what sort of narratives could possibly arise from attempts by women to take charge of their own lives. Where mobility was the preserve of men (Robert travels wherever he likes), what kind of unencumbered movement could lead out of the infantilising stasis of the early chapters? One option for Edna's tale would be to turn in horror from what she had done back to her children and family life (a motif wittily sent up by Stevie Smith in *Novel on Yellow Paper*). Another would be to run away with Robert and live a new life. It is a comment on the reader's share in the creation of narrative meaning that Edna's suicide could be seen either as the punishment allotted for transgression ('the wages of sin is death'), or, less schematically, as the only way out of an intolerable situation, and a family life which has become a prison.

> The children appeared before her like antagonists who had overcome her,
> who had overpowered and sought to drag her into the soul's slavery for
> the rest of her days. But she knew a way to elude them. (p.189)

The end of the novel represents an attempt to solve a contradiction posed by the society in which Edna lives. Within the social forms available, Edna's need for freedom can only lead her to repetition: a sexual pairing with another man.

Within the social forms available: our pursuit of the narrative outcome leads us (however sketchily) back from our own contemporary reading of *The Awakening* to history, and the context from which Edna Pontellier's story springs. For indeed a social situation is sketched in the novel, a world of banking, shops, making a fortune, servants, the Creole families, lightly brushed in. And it is this world which the contemporary reader is likely to find least easy to cope with. It is not, however, merely decorative, and even a brief attempt to understand the story needs to pay attention to the system within which the Pontelliers, Robert Lebrun, and the others operate. If one moment of a reading has to be reading for our own time, and licenses us to look for those issues that concern us now, another has to respect the difference of a vanished era.

The social order of the novel is likely to strike the contemporary reader as deeply objectionable: the nameless 'quadroon' who does all the serious looking after of the children, and who 'sat for hours... patient as a savage' for Edna to paint (think what a history of racial oppression and insult lurks *there*), the maids, the conspicuous consumption, the paying of afternoon calls. ('A light-colored mulatto boy, in dress coat, and bearing a silver tray for the reception of cards, admitted [the callers]. A maid, in white fluted cap, offered the callers liqueur, coffee, or chocolate, as they might desire...') These things confront any reader of the novel: Edna, in one respect a figure of liberation, is at the same time one of the oppressors herself. This contradiction is at the heart of the novel, and our attempts as readers to negotiate it will re-enact the conflicts of the text itself. The world of conspicuous consumption that Edna Pontellier occupies largely conceals the labour by which the wealth of the Pontelliers and their class is created. In the end, her tragedy is that she is of her time, and, like the rest of us, being of her time cannot altogether think her way out of it. Dimly aware of the emptiness of her situation, filled with longings for which she cannot find a name, yet implicated in the mode of being of a whole society, there is no magic solution. Part of the hardness and the realism of the novel lies, it seems to me, in Chopin's refusal, through engineering Robert's ambiguous departure, to treat romance as a way out.

If too many things bind Edna Pontellier to the social order of which she is a part, the novel's judgement on that enclosure and that limitation is perhaps hinted at once again through art. In her last moments Edna imagines Mlle Reisz's laughter:

> And you call yourself an artist! What pretentions, Madame! The artist must possess the courageous soul that dares and defies.

We have already seen that art codes liberation through expression, and it is back to her sketches that Edna has turned as a way out of the ennui of her life. If the novel maintains, as I think it does, her superficiality and lack of stamina as an artist then it is up to us readers whether we see this as a judgment on Edna in some essential sense ('she' is not up to what she really needs to do) or whether we believe that the weight of the superficiality which surrounds her is simply too much for one woman on her own to break out of. Painting may not be enough to liberate her, but has, at all events, permitted her dreaming space in which to get in touch with her own desire (pp.96–7).

At the end, the image of Edna casting off the 'unpleasant, pricking garments' and standing for the first time in her life naked in the open air, recalls (the subtle echoes of this book keep sounding back and forth) the metaphor of social self as garment. In Chapter Nineteen, Mr Pontellier, confronted with the uncomfortable phenomenon of a partner who is beginning to change her life has wondered whether 'his wife were not growing a little unbalanced mentally'. The narrator comments that he

> could see plainly that she was not herself. That is, he could not see that she was becoming herself and daily casting aside that fictitious self which we assume like a garment with which to appear before the world. (p.96)

This novel can offer no way other than suicide for Edna to escape from the false self she occupies; there is no alternative clothing; her society denies her a new role. Unless, as the last page seems to suggest, there is a way through art. And it is indeed through art that Edna's story is cast and made available to readers to perform their own imaginative work upon. The return to the sea and to nothingness mirrors that cycle re-enacted in the reading. We know that every time we pick up the book Edna Pontellier will live – and die – again. Every time she does so, she adds anew to the sum of human vitality.

Part Two

Introduction

Let me state both what this 'reader's guide' section aims to do, and what it cannot do. Above all, this section of the book is not intended to stand on its own; it is offered as a sequel to and in the context of the main text. The suggestions it makes follow up the arguments put forward there. The intention is to offer interested readers a guide to texts which may mesh with their therapeutic and counselling concerns. This is ironic in view of the persistent argument advanced before that texts ought not to be viewed mimetically, as 'about' particular topics or concerns. I have struggled with this irony: but in the end it seemed necessary to proceed by way of topics which could immediately be perceived as useful.

This usefulness needs to be approached with two precautions; first (and for reasons I hope adequately explained earlier on) no text can ever be 'about' a single topic. Meanings are generated in the dialogue between reader and texts, and meanings are inevitably plural rather than singular. Further, we need to 'hear' texts as a play of voices rather than a monologue, and these voices may overlap or even contradict each other. These, we might say, are the kind of narratives that might be needed to do justice to a particular subject matter. So my aim has not been simply to compile a list of authors who have written 'about' topics likely to come up in counselling or therapy, but to point to texts whose form, and whose manner of telling permit the reader to engage anew even with familiar subject matter.

The second observation concerns the life of the reader. There is no direct circuit from text to problem that by-passes the reader's own inner space. The circuit lies through the imagination of the reader/counsellor, through his or her empathy, attentiveness to language, nuance and narration, his or her consideration for story as social act. Such capacities, I would argue, depend upon the counsellor's willingness to allow his or her imagination to be fed, to make psychic room for play and (in the fullest sense) recreation. If I have offered some broad thematic headings, it is in the hope that you will find in the readings proposed both insight and enrichment.

It is important to make quite clear that the choice of authors and texts reflects my own reading and preoccupations. This is a personal list. I have made no attempt to pursue a phantom of inclusiveness, or even of 'obvious' texts. Some of the suggestions are obvious, others, I hope, not. There are considerable gaps in the areas represented, gaps which reflect both the defects of my own knowledge, and the inevitable problems of making a selection of any kind. The selection is intended to point onwards and outwards. I hope to encourage you to your own voyages of exploration. To that end, this is a pluralist selection: no one author or tradition is a guaranteed source of wisdom, though readings of different authors should complement each other.

The list of themes and the list of authors may be used in conjunction with each other, although the list of authors could stand on its own. In each entry, minimal information about the author is followed by a brief statement of the underlying themes and questions which prompted inclusion here, and suggestions for reading. Where a writer's work is bulky, I have suggested a starting place and follow up. I hope that both lists will lead to further reading which cannot be predicted in advance. The list of topics is obviously not exhaustive. Many readers may be disappointed by the absence of themes; I hope that this absence will spur them to compile their own lists. The suggestions which follow each entry point towards examples of texts where that topic occupies a good deal of the foreground.

This may appear in some ways a dreary list – serious themes seriously treated. I cannot conceal my own belief that most of the literature to which it is worth giving attentive reading is of a serious nature, and I have sometimes been accused of teaching courses on doom and gloom. Two brief thoughts about this: one is that in a society whose most influential media are largely given to trivia and to manic mirth, it may be that it is left to our novelists, playwrights and poets to speak of what our culture prefers to deny. Second, that when literature does deal with pain, loss, or thwarted human effort there may take place in the reader an effect long ago noticed by those who tried to account for the pleasure afforded by tragedy. Exposure to the medium, far from being depressing, calls into being regenerative mental energy.

NOTE ON EDITIONS

Wherever possible, I have given a paperback edition available at the time of going to press. However, recent rapid take-overs in the publishing world, and the movement of series into different imprints may mean that you do not always find a book listed with the publisher you expected. Thus, for instance, Doris Lessing, who was published by Triad Granada (subsequently Triad Grafton), moved to Picador and is now mostly to be found in Flamingo.

Topics

Few poems or novels are devoted to a single 'problem': novels in particular tend to contextualise psychological themes within overlapping social dynamics. It is, of course, part of their value that they direct our attention to the larger dramas – open or covert – within which the problems of individuals or families come into prominence and take on meaning. The reader is caught up in these dramas through a process akin to transference, but is at the same time free to step outside the situation to reflect on what is happening. Reading, we might say destabilises our tendency to think of conditions or symptoms as *nouns*, and offer us the possibility of re-framing them as *verbs* – as human actions and processes, rather than abstract entities.

The novels and poems listed are intended as samples of the wealth of material available. Anyone's reading will soon lead them to accumulate instances of their own.

Where no reference follows a title, you will find the work in question in the list of suggested authors.

ABUSE (of children and young people)
Fiction

Alice Walker, *The Color Purple*; Christina Stead, *The Man who Loved Children*; Iain Banks, *The Wasp Factory* (Abacus).

ADOLESCENCE
Fiction

James Joyce, *Portrait of the Artist as a Young Man*; Carson McCullers, *The Member of the Wedding*; Angela Carter, *The Magic Toyshop*; Paula Marshall, *Brown Girl, Brownstones* (Virago); L.P. Hartley, *The Go-Between*; J.D. Salinger, *Catcher in the Rye* (Penguin); Alain-Fournier, *Le Grand Meaulnes* (Penguin); Jeanette Winterson, *Oranges are Not the Only Fruit* (Pandora).

AGEING
Non-fiction (edited interviews)
Ronald Blythe, *The View in Winter* (Allen Lane).

Fiction
Paul Scott, *Staying On* (Granada); Ellen Glasgow, *The Sheltered Life*; Tillie Olsen's title story 'Tell Me a Riddle', Grace Paley 'A Conversation with my Father' in *Enormous Changes at the Last Minute* (Virago), and Chekhov's tale 'A Boring Story'. Bobbie Ann Mason's story 'Nancy Culpepper' (in *Shiloh and Other Stories*).

Poems
Jenny Joseph, 'Warning' (in ed. Jeni Couzyn, *The Bloodaxe Book of Contemporary Women Poets*). Also in (ed.) Couzyn are Elizabeth Jennings' 'Rembrandt's Late Self Portraits' and Ruth Fainlight's 'It Must'.

ALCOHOLISM
Fiction
Malcolm Lowry's novel *Under the Volcano* (Penguin), or Tillie Olsen's story 'Hey Sailor, What Ship' (in *Tell Me a Riddle*).

ANGER
Fiction
James Kelman, *A Disaffection*.

Poems
William Blake's 'The Poison Tree' (from *Songs of Experience*) and Stevie Smith's 'Anger's Freeing Power'.

BEREAVEMENT see 'mourning'

BULLYING
Fiction
Margaret Atwood, *Cat's Eye*.

Poem
Edwin Muir, 'The Ballad of Hector in Hades' (and see Muir's *Autobiography*).

CHILDHOOD
Fiction
Dickens, *David Copperfield*, and *Great Expectations*; Charlotte Brontë, *Jane Eyre*; Lawrence, *Sons and Lovers*; Katherine Mansfield's stories 'Prelude', 'Sun and

Moon', and 'The Doll's House'; and Christina Stead, *The Man Who Loved Children*. (cf. 'Families').

Cultural Difference – Experiencing
Fiction

Jean Rhys (e.g. stories like 'Let them call it Jazz'); Nadine Gordimer, *A World of Strangers* and *Burger's Daughter*, and in stories like 'The Night the Favourite came in' and 'Abroad'. Grace Paley (e.g. stories in *Enormous Changes at the Last Minute*, Virago). People who return to communities and find themselves become strangers figure in Arnold Wesker's play *Roots* and Thomas Hardy's novel *The Return of the Native*. Tsitsi Dangarembga's novel *Nervous Conditions* (Women's Press) is a vivid account of moving between a traditional African society and a westernised education.

Cultural Norms

Do you go along with the norms and values of your group or find the courage to challenge them?

Fiction

Doris Lessing, *The Grass is Singing*; Marge Piercy, *Woman on the Edge of Time*; Arthur Koestler, *Darkness at Noon* (Penguin); Milan Kundera, *The Joke* (Penguin); Heinrich Böll, *The Clown* (Marion Boyars).

Drama
Arthur Miller, *The Crucible*.

Death (see also 'mourning')
Stories
Tolstoy, 'The Death of Ivan Illych', and Tillie Olsen 'Tell Me a Riddle'.

Poems
Emily Dickinson, 'I heard a fly buzz when I died'; Denise Levertov, 'Death Psalm', Jeni Couzyn, 'A Death in Winter' in *Bloodaxe Book of Contemporary Women Poets*; Jon Silkin ('Death of a Son' in *Collected Poems*, Dent), and Stephen Spender 'Elegy for Margaret' in *Collected Poems* (Faber).

Depression

An inadequate term to cover a variety of more or less debilitating emotional states. The subject became of great interest in the romantic era and after, though the condition clearly has affinities with that known previously in religious terms as doubt or the loss of faith. For that reason a seventeenth-century poem such as

George Herbert's 'The Flower' (in *The Penguin Book of Metaphysical Verse*) is extremely relevant. In the same volume you will also find John Donne's beautiful 'Nocturnall upon St. Lucies Day'. A number of fine poems from the Romantic era address the subject of the loss of creative and joyful powers, and the associated feeling of worthlessness, most notably Coleridge's 'Dejection, an Ode'. Other poems include the group of so-called 'Terrible Sonnets' of Gerard Manley Hopkins (they begin with the sonnet 'No worst there is none', nos. 65–69 in the *Collected Poems*, Oxford), William Carlos Williams' 'These' (in *Selected Poems*, Penguin), Edwin Muir's 'Comfort in Self-Despite', Sylvia Plath's 'The Moon and the Yew Tree', and Robert Lowell's 'Skunk Hour' (*Life Studies*, Faber). Margaret Drabble's novel *The Waterfall* (Penguin) seems to me to give a very vivid account of prolonged state of depression.

DESIRE

It is tempting to say that there are so many representations of sexual desire in literature that one despairs of offering meaningful suggestions. The heavy coding which has often been required in writing about this subject poses thought-provoking questions about the uses of difficulty and the power of suggestion. Can a repressed age write more energetically about desire? A rather patriarchal point of view is both proposed and undercut in Shakespeare's Sonnet 129 ('Th'expense of spirit in a waste of shame'). From recent times I would cite D.H. Lawrence – both in poems and fiction – as one of the pioneers in forging a written language for desire. I have to add that his pioneering work goes with some polemical and highly questionable views on man–woman relations. The significance you attach to desire is itself a political matter, and André Brink's *States of Emergency* (Flamingo) is an attempt to locate it as a disruptive but also distracting force within a political sphere. Compare Lewis Nkosi's *Mating Birds* (Flamingo) which subverts and politicises stereotypes about relationships between black men and white women. AIDS and a wider awareness of the politics of sexuality mean that it is no longer possible to celebrate desire as an unambiguously liberating force. From an era when it was possible to be a lot less ambiguous about sexual emancipation, see Alison Lurie's novel *Love and Friendship* (Abacus) and Marge Piercy's novel *Braided Lives* (Penguin). Liz Lochhead's poems ebulliently undermine some old tales, e.g. in 'The Grimm Sisters' in *Dreaming Frankenstein* (Polygon). Also Cynthia Fuller's Poem 'Desire' in *Moving Towards Light* (Flambard).

DEVIANCE (see also 'Outsiders')
Fiction

Herman Melville's story 'Bartleby' (in *Billy Budd, Sailor, and Other Stories*, Penguin); Dostoyevsky's novels *Notes from Underground*, and *Crime and Punishment*; Athol Fugard's novel *Tsotsi* (Penguin); J.M. Coetzee's novel *The Life and Times of Michael*

K.; Ian McEwan's story 'Butterflies' (in *First Love, Last Rites*, Picador) and Jean Genet's unclassifiable work *The Thief's Journal* (Penguin).

Drama
Georg Büchner, *Woyzeck* (Methuen).

ENDURANCE
Fiction
Willa Cather *O Pioneers!*; Ellen Glasgow, *Barren Ground*; Russell Hoban, *Riddley Walker*; Doris Lessing, *Memoirs of a Survivor* (Picador). Also perhaps Katherine Mansfield's story 'Pictures'.

Drama
Brecht, *Mother Courage*.

Non-Fiction
Agnes Smedley's *Daughter of Earth* (Virago) (autobiography).

FAMILIES
Fiction
The following novels explore familial themes from different angles: D.H. Lawrence, *Sons and Lovers*; Virginia Woolf, *To the Lighthouse*; Christina Stead, *The Man who Loved Children*; Beryl Bainbridge, *A Quiet Life*; Eudora Welty, *The Optimist's Daughter*; Thomas Mann, *Buddenbrooks* (Penguin). Also stories by Eudora Welty ('Why I Live at the PO'), Alice Munro ('The Progress of Love' in *The Progress of Love*, Flamingo/Fontana), Grace Paley, 'The Used-Boy Raisers' (in *The Little Disturbances of Man*, Virago), and Bobbie Ann Mason ('Drawing Names'). These all treat the members of the family as equally caught up in family dynamics. For an account of more overt manipulation see Henry James's *Washington Square*, and Molly Keane's *Loving without Tears* (Virago). See also Eugene O' Neill's bleak play *Long Day's Journey into Night* (Cape).

GENDER (and oppression)
Fiction
Doris Lessing, *The Summer Before the Dark*; Fay Weldon, *Praxis* (Hodder); Pat Barker, *Union Street*; Zoë Fairbairns, *Benefits* (Virago); Marge Piercy, *Woman on the Edge of Time*.

GRIEF (and see 'Death', 'Mourning')
Wordsworth's poem 'Surprised by Joy', Seamus Heaney 'The Summer of Lost Rachel' (in *The Haw Lantern*).

INSTITUTIONALISATION
Fiction

Victor Serge, *Men in Prison* (Writers and Readers); Thomas Mann, *The Magic Mountain*; Ken Kesey, *One Flew over the Cuckoo's Nest* (Picador); Alexander Solzhenytsin, *One Day in the Life of Ivan Denisovich* (Penguin). The subject receives a more allegorical while chilling treatment in Kafka's story 'In the Penal Colony'. Outside the realist tradition, but worth reading if you're prepared to come to terms with its genre is Herman Hesse's novel *The Glass Bead Game* (Penguin).

Poems

Poems by Ken Smith in his collection *Wormwood*, e.g. 'Timekeeper'.

INTERVENTION

By what right do people (friends, family or professionals) intervene in other people's lives? What happens when they do? One would think that literature would abound with attempts to examine this problem, but while lots of more or less well-meant advice goes astray, I can think of few examples where the subject becomes thematic. The topic fascinated Henry James, and Ralph Touchett's interference in Isabel Archer's life (*The Portrait of a Lady*) is an excellent example. It is also a topic that recurs in Henrik Ibsen's plays, for example in *The Wild Duck*. In a loose sense I suppose that it is also the subject of Jane Austen's *Emma*. There are some writers of short fiction who have been drawn to this problem: Flannery O'Connor in stories such as 'The Lame Shall Enter First' (in *Everything that Rises Must Converge*); Grace Paley in 'Distance' (in *Enormous Changes at the Last Minute*, Virago); Nadine Gordimer in 'Which New Era Would That Be?'; and Jane Gardam in 'Swan' (in *Showing the Flag*, Abacus).

JEALOUSY

Shakespeare's *A Winter's Tale*, Tolstoy's story *The Kreutzer Sonata*, and Julian Barnes' novel *Before She Met Me* (Picador).

LANGUAGE AND CLASS

In a class society, dialect and sociolect are inevitably tangled with judgments about social status and even human worth. A number of novelists have raised the subject of the tension between the language you grew up in and the language you are educated into in novels which take an autobiographical structure. D.H. Lawrence (e.g. *Sons and Lovers*), and David Storey (*Saville*, Penguin) are examples. One poet who has forcefully addressed this subject is Tony Harrison, most of whose *School of Eloquence* is relevant. Examples would be: 'On Not Being Milton', 'Wordlists', 'Them and [Uz]', though the whole collection (most of it in *Selected Poems*) should be read.

LONELINESS
Fiction

Jean Rhys, *After Leaving Mr Mackenzie* and *Wide Sargasso Sea*. Katherine Mansfield, too, had a go at the subject in stories such as 'Life of Ma Parker' and 'Miss Brill', James Joyce in 'A Painful Case' (in *Dubliners*), Ian McEwan in 'Conversation with a Cupboard Man' (in *First Love, Last Rites*, Picador), and James Kelman in 'Not Not While the Giro'. Nathaniel Hawthorne (1804–1864), stories for example 'The Minister's Black Veil', 'The Birth-mark', or other tales in *Selected Tales and Sketches* (Penguin).

Poems

A couple of long poems in particular seem appropriate – Coleridge's 'The Ancient Mariner' and Roy Fisher's prose poem 'The Ship's Orchestra' (in Poems 1950–1980, Oxford). As to shorter poems: there are Stevie Smiths 'Not Waving but Drowning' and 'Do Take Muriel Out', or read around in Emily Dickinson, or Ken Smith's *Wormwood* volume.

MADNESS
Fiction

Doris Lessing, *Briefing for a Descent into Hell*, David Storey, *Pasmore* (Penguin). Antonia White: see *Beyond the Glass*, or the short story 'The House of Clouds' reprinted in *The Secret Self 2* (Dent). In very different keys, you could explore Shakespeare's *King Lear* or Iain Sinclair's *White Chappell, Scarlet Facings* (Picador).

MASCULINITY
Fiction

Ian McEwan (*The Child in Time*, Picador), Martin Amis (*London Fields*, Penguin), Jeff Torrington (*Swing Hammer Swing*, Secker and Warburg). Also James Kelman, for example his story 'Lassies Are Trained That Way' in *The Burn*. From an earlier generation, it is also instructive to read between the lines of Ford Madox Ford's novel *The Good Soldier* (Penguin).

MARRIAGE

There are thousands of marriages in literature, and the comedic tradition means that one strand of the novel (the dominant strand for much of the nineteenth century) centred on courtship and marriage which in turn provided the plot with a resolution. More to our purpose, some novelists have taken as a subject the nature and dynamics of a long term relationship between two people, and Tolstoy's *Anna Karenin* provides deeply moving examples. D.H. Lawrence's stories frequently figure the wordless marriage – two people locked in a pattern about which they have no language to talk (e.g. 'The Odour of Chrysanthemums').

Antonia White's *The Lost Traveller*, and *The Sugar House* explore a couple's attempts to stabilise a destructive relationship. Marriage is addressed in numerous short stories, for example James Joyce's 'A Little Cloud' (in *Dubliners*), and Bobbie Ann Mason's 'Shiloh' (in the collection of that name). One attempt to tackle marital breakdown is Alison Lurie's *The War between the Tates* (Abacus).

Poets

Among poets, see Denise Levertov's 'The Ache of Marriage' and 'The Marriage'; Elaine Feinstein, 'Marriage' (in *The Bloodaxe Book of Contemporary Women Poets*), Robert Lowell 'To speak of the woe that is in marriage' (*Life Studies*, Faber), and David Constantine 'As our bloods separate' in *A Brightness to Cast Shadows* (Bloodaxe).

Drama

A harrowing account of the potential destructive capacity of couples can be found in Edward Albee's play *Who's Afraid of Virginia Woolf?* (Penguin).

MEANINGLESSNESS

Probably the whole of Samuel Beckett's work is relevant, although I would pick out the short play *Not I*, and the longer play *Waiting for Godot* (both Faber). Harold Pinter's plays provide another example, for instance *The Birthday Party*. See also Kafka's novel *The Trial*, and Sylvia Plath's poem 'Insomniac'.

MEMORY – COMING TO TERMS WITH

A recurrent topic of fiction – as of life – is the question of how you deal with painful and difficult memories. Tidying them out of the way or outright repression doesn't always work, and when it does has undesirable side-effects. There are many literary examples of the return of unwanted memories. Texts where the question of how to cope with powerful memories bulks large include Ellen Glasgow's novel *The Sheltered Life*, L.P. Hartley's novel *The Go Between* (Penguin), and Margaret Atwood's *Cat's Eye*. It is also a theme of several of Arthur Miller's plays, for example *The Price*. Regret, the bleak realisation that you cannot re-run the past and do things better is the subject of a lot of Thomas Hardy's poetry. Look especially at the *Poems of 1912–13*. Although I have not generally included novels written for young people, I cannot avoid mentioning Margaret Mahy's remarkable *Memory* (Penguin/Puffin Plus). The 1980s 'postmodernist' preoccupation with narrative and its unreliability led to some remarkable novels about the constructive and re-organising powers of memory, for example Kazuo Ishiguro's *The Artist of the Floating World*, and *The Remains of the Day* (both Faber).

MEN'S RELATIONSHIPS (and see 'masculinity')

Until fairly recently, you had to read novels 'against the grain' to decipher what they were saying about this subject. Male homosocial bonds were so tied up with power over others that male writers saw them as nothing remarkable. There are lots of scattered instances of affection in relationships, for example in Lawrence (like the relationship of Birkin and Gerald in *Women in Love*). For a more self-conscious re-working, see Julian Barnes' novel *Talking it Over* (Picador). The general silence is patently cultural, and arises from a culture where the making and maintenance of relationships with family and friends has broadly been seen as the woman's role. Add to that the general taboo on representing work – the space where male relationships have typically been formed. Conrad's ships provide one way round that taboo, and male relationships are foregrounded in stories such as 'The Secret Sharer'. There is a portrait of the relations between brothers in Bruce Chatwin's novel *On The Black Hill* (Picador), and a powerful analysis of the bonding of males through banter and destructive humour in Trevor Griffiths' play *Comedians* (Faber). On explicitly gay relationships, see David Leavitt's novels, for example *The Lost Language of Cranes* and *Equal Affections*, or Andrew Halloran's *Dancer from the Dance* (all Penguin). E.M. Forster's posthumous novel *Maurice* (Penguin) throws light on the terrible strain placed on the gay novelist who has no public forum.

MOURNING
Poems

Tony Harrison's poems on his mother and father (*School of Eloquence*); Elaine Feinstein 'Dad' (in *Bloodaxe Book of Contemporary Women Poets*); Seamus Heaney 'Clearances' (in *The Haw Lantern*); Allen Ginsberg 'Kaddish for Naomi Ginsberg' (in *Poems*, Viking); David Constantine 'In Memoriam 8571 Private J.W. Gleave' (in *A Brightness to Cast Shadows*, Bloodaxe).

OPPRESSION (see also 'Gender' and 'Racial Discrimination')

The literature that has formed the staple of the 'English' curriculum has tended to stay away from overtly political themes (at least those more recent than the seventeenth century), and there has been an influential critical assumption that protest writing (unless it was war poetry) must be bad writing. This position is changing with the wide currency of politicised women's and black writing. To some extent the two latter themes converge in South Africa – see for example Nadine Gordimer's novel *Burger's Daughter*, or Lewis Nkosi's *Mating Birds* (Flamingo). If we are looking for responses to social and political repression, the European Jewish traditions give us, for example, the stories of Isaac Bashevis Singer (many in Penguin, including *Collected Stories* and *The Death of Methuselah*). On the subject of class, and within a British tradition we might look to a classic like Robert Tressell's novel *The Ragged Trousered Philanthropists* (Harper Collins), Harold Heslop's novel *Last Cage Down* (Wishart Books) or Raymond Williams' novel *Border Country* (Hogarth). In Britain in the 1970s and early 1980s there was a resurgence of political theatre – look out for plays by Howard Brenton, Edward Bond, Caryl Churchill, Trevor Griffiths, or David Hare. Television is beyond the scope of this book, but Alan Bleasdale's series *Boys from the Blackstuff* makes a powerful addition to the accounts of the enduring power of class.

OUTSIDERS (see 'Deviance')

Dostoyevsky's novel *Notes from Underground*, Camus's novel *The Outsider* (Penguin), Brecht's play *The Good Person of Szechuan*, and Kafka's *Metamorphosis*. Also stories by Jean Rhys in *Tigers are Better Looking*.

PANIC

Edwin Muir's 'Ballad of Hector in Hades' (interestingly discussed in his *Autobiography*). Some Emily Dickinson, and some Plath (e.g. 'Insomniac') seem to edge on this subject. Jean Rhys has a lot to say about minds on the edge of panic – see for example 'The Edge of the River' in *Tigers are Better Looking*. Chekhov's 'A Boring Story' contains what appears to be an account of a panic attack.

PARENTING

Two contrasting celebrations of the very young are Coleridge's poem 'Frost at Midnight' and Sylvia Plath's 'Nick and the Candlestick'. Jackie Kay's poems 'Whilst Leila Sleeps' and 'I Try My Absolute Best' (in *The Adoption Papers*, Bloodaxe) take a rather more wry look. The triangular dynamics of father, mother, and child are the subject of John Updike's story 'Should Wizard Hit Mommie' (in *Pigeon Feathers and Other Stories*, Penguin). A more retrospective reflection forms the substance of Tillie Olsen's story 'I Stand Here Ironing' (in *Tell Me a Riddle*), while finding yourself the father of a young man who appears to belong to a totally different culture forms the subject of R.K. Narayan's *The Vendor of Sweets* (Penguin). Christine Park and Caroline Heaton have edited *Close Company* (Virago), a volume of stories on the subject of mothers and daughters. See also Grace Paley's story 'A Subject of Childhood' in *The Little Disturbances of Man* (Virago), Anne Stevenson's poem 'With My Sons at Boarhills' in (ed.) Blake Morrison and Andrew Motion *The Penguin Book of Contemporary British Poetry*, Cynthia Fuller's 'To My Sons' in *Moving Towards Light* (Flambard), and Gareth Reeves' 'Travels with my Daughter' in *Real Stories* (Carcanet). Adoption figures prominently in Jackie Kay's *The Adoption Papers* (see above), and David Cook's novel *Second Best* (Faber).

RACIAL DISCRIMINATION (and see 'Oppression')

Much important work here has come out of the United States and South Africa, though there is a thriving British school of Black Poetry, usefully represented in Fred d'Aguiar's section of the Paladin *New British Poetry*, and in (ed.) E.A. Markham, *Hinterland, Caribbean Poetry from the West Indies and Britain* (Bloodaxe). For a start with the American work you might turn to the first volume of Maya Angelou's autobiography (*I Know Why the Caged Bird Sings*), Ralph Ellison's novel *The Invisible Man* (Penguin), novels by Toni Morrison, like *Sula* and *Beloved* and Alice Walker's stories in *In Love and Trouble*. Lewis Nkosi's *Mating Birds* would be an introduction to the South African work. Many of Flannery O'Connor's stories (e.g. in *Everything Which Rises Must Converge*) examine the situation of whites trying to come to terms with changes in racist world views, as to some extent does Ellen Douglas' novel *Can't Quit You Baby* (Virago).

SIBLING RELATIONS

There are so many examples in fiction, that selection is very difficult. You could turn to George Eliot's *The Mill on the Floss*, D.H. Lawrence's *Sons and Lovers*, Beryl Bainbridge's *A Quiet Life*, or Iain Banks' *The Wasp Factory* (Abacus). Relations between sisters form the theme of Louisa Alcott's *Little Women*, which is far more than 'just' a children's novel.

TRADITIONAL COMMUNITIES – BREAK UP OF

While we should not erase specificity in pursuit of supposed universal themes, it seems to me that accounts from different times and places help us gain a grasp of widely various but in some ways parallel phenomena. So, for example, it might make a lot of sense to set alongside each other the Nigerian novelist Chinua Achebe's novel *Things Fall Apart*, Thomas Hardy's *The Woodlanders*, Kazuo Ishiguro's *The Artist of the Floating World* (Faber), Isaac Bashevis Singer's stories, or Arnold Wesker's play *Roots*. This is a subject which leads us out across the borderlines of fiction, and I would add Carlo Levi's memoir *Christ Stopped at Eboli* (Penguin), and John Berger's reflection *Pig Earth* (Writers and Readers). Lewis Grassic Gibbon's great trilogy *A Scots Quair* (Canongate; or Penguin) is a deeply moving account of the passing of a traditional society, as (in a different place and mode) is Winifred Holtby's *South Riding*. But you do not need to come from a rural or peasant culture to experience such an historical upheaval: there are also accounts of profound change in urban communities in (for example) Sid Chaplin's novels (e.g. *The Day of the Sardine* and *The Watchers and the Watched*, Scorpion), and plays by Alan Plater (*Close the Coalhouse Door*, Methuen) and Cecil Taylor (*A Nightingale Sang in the Eldon Square*, Methuen). Finally, social change affects as well those who are materially better off, and the deep ambiguity of the subject (you can mourn even an iniquitous social order) juts up through Chekhov's plays, or a novel like Ellen Glasgow's *The Sheltered Life*.

UNEMPLOYMENT
Fiction

Walter Greenwood, *Love on the Dole* (Penguin); many of James Kelman's stories, for example in *Not Not While the Giro*, and *Greyhound for Breakfast*.

WOMEN'S RELATIONSHIPS
Fiction

As nineteenth century examples Elizabeth Gaskell's novels *Cranford*, and *Wives and Daughters*, also Charlotte Brontë's *Villette*. More recently, note Doris Lessing's work, especially, in this connection, *The Golden Notebook*, Marilyn French's *The Women's Room*, and Jeanette Winterson's *Oranges are Not the Only Fruit* (Pandora).

WORK

Paid work is an elusive subject in literature. Among the novels which have tackled the subject are Harold Heslop's *Last Cage Down* (Wishart Books), Sid Chaplin's stories in *The Thin Seam* (out of print, but you might find it in a library), James Kelman's *The Busconductor Hines*, and some of his stories, Primo Levi's *The Wrench* (Abacus). The macho temper of much shop floor work is explored in Fred Voss's poems *Goodstone* (Bloodaxe). See also John Harvey, *The Plate Shop* (also out of print).

Guide to Authors

Anthologies – of Fiction – short stories. Anthologies are often a good way of sampling a variety of authors. Three recent collections should be included here. The two volumes of *The Secret Self: Short Stories by Women*, edited by Hermione Lee (Dent), and *Close Company: Stories of Mothers and Daughters*, edited by Christine Park and Caroline Heaton (Virago).

Poetry, Contemporary There are a number of anthologies which represent recent work. These include (eds.) Blake Morrison and Andrew Motion, *The Penguin Book of Contemporary British Poetry*. Rather wider in scope, and more representative of small press work are (eds.) Andrew Crozier and Tim Longville, *A Various Art* (Carcanet), and (eds.) Gillian Allnut and others *The New British Poetry* (Paladin). One of the publishing successes of recent years has been the Newcastle-based firm Bloodaxe Books, who now have one of the leading poetry lists. This includes a lot of fine European work as well as many of the best contemporary British poets. Note in particular two of their anthologies: (ed.) Jeni Couzyn, *The Bloodaxe Book of Contemporary Women Poets*, and (ed.) Neil Astley, *Poetry With an Edge*.

Achebe, Chinua (b. 1930) Nigerian novelist. The problematic of CA's work revolves around the contrary tension of oral narrative and of writing in a 'western' literary tradition. Appropriately, his recurrent topic is the destruction of traditional communities under the joint onslaught of colonisation and western values. While in one sense his novels are 'about' West Africa, they are also 'about' those at the receiving end of other people's missions, and the effect upon structures of feeling of being caught up in rapid historical change. For the reader they open up the problem of entering imaginatively into other cultures.

> Starting place: *Things Fall Apart* (Heinemann) (also in *The African Trilogy* [Picador])
>
> Further Reading: *Anthills of the Savannah* (Picador)

Akhmatova, Anna (1889–1966) There are ethical questions about the spectatorship of other peoples' horrors, yet the horrors which AA addresses are close enough to the core events of twentieth century history for us to need to be able to see what kind of artistic response could be made to them.

Selected Poems (trans. Richard McKane) (Bloodaxe)

Angelou, Maya (b. 1928) U.S. novelist. Has become widely known in this country for her autobiography, especially the first volume, *I Know Why the Caged Bird Sings* (Virago). This both articulates and gives a form to the rise of black consciousness, and shapes a way of representing the struggle of some one trapped between cultures to make her way in one without selling out the other. It is thus possible to read it (and without minimising the specificity of black experience) for the light it sheds upon the tensions of class allegiance or between the culture of your parental family and that you grow up into. Her work vividly evokes experiences of childhood, schooling, and adolescence. Autobiography is in any case interesting for the way in which it processes your past and shapes it into tellable narrative. Autobiography has more in common with fiction than is often recognised.

Atwood, Margaret (b. 1939) MA's protagonists seem drawn back to a search for origins, looking for the missing bits of the jigsaw in the past. They struggle with the power of memory and its hold over your life. She is a vivid novelist of growing up, specifically as a woman and in the Canada of the 1940s and 1950s. On the other hand, that description boxes her in, and she has created a form of discourse for talking about the compromises and camouflage which constitute one of the routes by which members of an oppressed group may attain some limited control over their own lives. Like a number of other women novelists (e.g. Lessing) she has not always found realism adequate to her concerns, and *The Handmaid's Tale* tells of a futuristic dystopia which acts as a measure of the contemporary trends she strives to elucidate. Domination and the refusal of victim role are topics which recur at all levels of MA's work, and *Cat's Eye* contains (among other things) a vivid account of childhood bullying.

> Starting places: *The Edible Woman, Life before Man*
> Further reading: *The Handmaid's Tale, Cat's Eye* (all Virago)

Bainbridge, Beryl (b. 1934) Deeply interested in the destructive forces implicit in apparently quite ordinary human situations in the home or at work. *A Quiet Life* (Fontana) is a rivetting study of the effects of unresolved family conflict on the lives of a brother and sister, particularly the brother, who attempts to cope with the pain by denial. It is also a study of the pain of living on the margins of social class.

Further Reading: *An Awfully Big Adventure* (Penguin)

Barker, Pat (b. 1943) Works on the problem of representing working class life (especially women's lives) without being drawn into either warm sentimentality or unmitigated awfulness. She deals with a serious cultural problem which is how 'unliterary' lives can be represented without being conventionalised. *Union Street* (Virago) (despite its metamorphosis into the film *Stanley and Iris*) is a sequence of interconnected stories which investigate the lack of choices but also the courage available to their women protagonists.

Bennett, Alan (b. 1934) Included here for his TV monologues, published as *Talking Heads* (BBC Books), a remarkable collection of speakers baffled by their own stories, and bit by bit undermining their own case. The reader/ listener is likely to be torn between 'seeing through' them, and the terrible pathos of their self deception. Insight into the frequently delusive nature of first person narrative.

Brecht, Bertolt (1898–1956) The current denigration of all BB stood for should not tempt us to ignore his work. The rather heterodox Marxism through to which he worked provided him with a powerful symbolic structure for articulating the dynamics of social existence. His characters do not have interiors in the novelistic sense, but they struggle to survive within a social formation dedicated to war and the appropriation of human energy as wealth. His 'alienation effect' (the reframing of familiar injustice in an unexpected way) still has the power to create shock and unease because it deliberately repells empathy and the pull of 'story', encouraging you to think out how the story might have been different. A useful corrective to the tendency to see all human problems as having their origins within the individual or the family.

Starting places: *Mother Courage; The Caucasian Chalk Circle*
Further reading: *The Good Person of Szechuan* (all Methuen)

Brontë, Charlotte (1816–55) CB's central problematic is of concern to anyone facing the problems of autonomy ringed around with social constraint. While she is particularly concerned with women's attempts to create their own roles, her attention to the deformation of the self in the attempt to break free has further applications. In *Villette* she threw over the attempt to solve the problem by recourse to romance. She strikingly deserves modern consideration for the way in which her speakers project dissociated parts of themselves onto split off voices.

> Starting Place: *Villette* (Penguin)
>
> Further reading: *Jane Eyre* (Penguin).

Brontë, Emily (1818–48) Though remembered largely for her novel *Wuthering Heights* (Penguin), EB was also a considerable poet. The dramatic speakers of her poetry might be compared with those of Christina Rossetti and Emily Dickinson. *Wuthering Heights* tantalises and often vexes readers by the number of levels at which it may be read, and through its narrative structure – the story is mediated through different narrators – it places the problems of interpretation firmly before us. It may be that it is its very enigmatic and baffling quality that is its value, enabling EB to investigate disruptive forces at the social and individual levels.

> There is a selection of her poems in *The Brontë Sisters: Selected Poems* (Carcanet)

Carter, Angela (1940–1992) Concerned with the way in which fantasy inter-sects with what we reassuringly think of as ordinary life. Fantasy for AC appears to be a way of exploring the possibility of evading the limiting and tyrannical bounds placed upon human potential by a patriarchal society. (It is however difficult sometimes to avoid the impression that she is simply playing pornogra-phy at its own game – humans and gruesome events are apt to become counters in her work.)

> Suggestion: *The Magic Toyshop* (Virago)

Cather, Willa (1873–1947) Difficult to pin down a central theme to WC's work. Two areas of great concern to her – community constructing itself on the American plains, and the damaging effects of enclosed relationships – are perhaps linked through her interest in the creative energy of women, and the ways in which that energy can be used or turned in upon itself.

Her prairie novels (e.g. *O Pioneers!*, *My Antonia*) foreground the community constructing itself a new history, but nevertheless living out patterns and memories brought from the old world. They represent a modern variation on the ancient theme of pastoral: the location of alternative values in a rural world. In them, place and descriptions of place often become a code for sexuality. WC's narratives are deceptively loose, springing surprises when you least expect them.

> Starting place: *My Antonia*
>
> Further reading: *O Pioneers!*, *My Mortal Enemy*, *A Lost Lady* (all Virago)

Chekhov, Anton (1860–1904) Russian dramatist and short story writer. As with all dramatists, it's worth looking out for productions, TV or live. Plays spring (literally and metaphorically) into 3D when performed, and can appear so thin on the page. AC is concerned with the shaping influence on human intentions and motivation of living in a social order that seems to have lost its rationale, and where old inequalities, having become drearily familiar, leak into all aspects of life. AC's characters are locked in their roles, stuck in the gap between self-rhetoric and achievement. Reading/seeing AC attunes you to hearing implication and nuance, the subtext of human dealings with one another. His protagonists experience a nostalgia for something they seem to have lost, and a longing for something they do not know how to gain, investing all their hope in a return to an imagined past state of things. The result is acute insight into the social economy of hope and lethargy.

> Suggested starting place: you could begin with any one of these plays. *Uncle Vanya; The Three Sisters; The Cherry Orchard* (Penguin).
>
> Further reading: stories – volumes published by Penguin and Oxford University Press.

Chopin, Kate (1850–1904) see Chapter 5

Coetzee, J.M. (b. 1940) More evidence for the extraordinary fecundity of the South African novel. His subjects are dispossession and marginality. In *The Life and Times of Michael K.* (Penguin) he addresses the problem of how to impute narrative to an outsider, some one who lacks the cultural resources that the literate community takes for granted. In *Waiting for the Barbarians* (Penguin) he moves into an imagined society, and explores the vulnerability of a culture from the standpoint of rather genteel privilege. Like some other imaginary domains, this land startles and invigorates the imagination, raising issues of responsibility, power, the forms of hope and pathos bequeathed by an imperial past.

Conrad, Joseph (1857–1924) Historically, JC stands at a point where he straddles both the onset of modernism, and the development of the adventure story/thriller. That some of his attitudes (e.g. on gender and race) are questionable, does not rule out reading him. Indeed as a general note, a 'resisting reading' of a text (reading it against the grain of its own values) can be a formative experience. JC is deeply interested in the growing up and initiation of young men, and his ships form microcosmic communities where leaders frequently fail to live up to the authority invested in them. Perhaps his subtext throughout is movement between cultures (he was himself Polish, adoptively English) and the voyages the individual undertakes in pursuit of authentic roles, and in pursuit of a reference community who will validate their lives. His narrators may perhaps parallel the counsellor who only half understands.

Starting place: stories in *'Twixt Land and Sea; Typhoon* (novella)

Further reading: *Heart of Darkness; The End of the Tether* (novella/story); *Nostromo* (novel) (all Penguin)

Dickens, Charles (1807–1870) A classic sufficiently well known probably not to need mention here. Worth, however, stressing that – while CD is frequently criticised for failing to grant his characters an interior world, this is probably not an appropriate criticism. Not only are his novels concerned with the obsessive patterns into which people become locked, but they can be envisaged as psychodramas in which split off and often fearful portions of the psyche interact. Often the tension so created is resolved by the expulsion (through death or humiliation) of the dissociated evil-doer. Such an internalising of CD isn't adequate either: the sheer scale of his novels dramatises the dynamic connections operating in the social world, the interlinking of the structures of experience in varied social settings. One way in might well be through his recurrent motive of the child wronged and oppressed by the adult world, and, conversely of the adult who finds it impossible to take up an adult identity.

Starting place: *Great Expectations*

Further reading: *David Copperfield; Bleak House; Hard Times* (all Penguin, among many other editions)

Dickinson, Emily (1830–1886) ED has recurred in these pages because it seems to me that her exploration of the problems of writing as a woman in nineteenth century America leads her into a voyage into the interior, of peculiar interest to those whose function is listening to people's accounts of their inner world. A lot of her supposed 'difficulty' seems to be the difficulty of finding a language for that world. She uses her isolation and the protestant tradition as the material for intensive reflection. Her poems work through their brevity, their enigmatic ellipsis, their surprising imagery, forcing the reader into a dialogue about the dramas of fear, loneliness, guilt, and the voices with which the inner spaces are peopled. Her poems need to be read and re-read before they start to thicken in the mind.

A Choice of Emily Dickinson's Verse (Faber); *Complete Poems* (Faber)

Dostoyevsky, Fyodor (1821–1881) The turbulent and nightmarish effect FD achieves derives both from the savage contradictions of nineteenth century Russian social life, and from his pushing his protagonists to the limit, stripping them to achieve maximum exposure. His novels concern themselves with those who either take themselves or are driven outside the security of recognised social position, and who are therefore forced to make major decisions without having patterns laid down for them. Under such conditions, and surrounded by debris of all sorts, they sometimes achieve an almost hallucinated lucidity. In the late twentieth century we perhaps need to take seriously his critique of the shibboleths of western enlightenment – progress, rationalism, science.

Starting place: *Crime and Punishment* (Penguin)

Further reading: *Notes from the Underground; The Brothers Karamazov, The Idiot* (all Penguin)

Eliot, George (pseudonym of Mary Ann Evans – 1819–1883) Deeply committed to the humanist programme of achieving social change through enlarging her readers' sympathy, GE is fascinated by the reciprocal relations between social forms (especially those of small provincial towns) and individual lives and intimate relationships. There is in her work a prominent tension between those who seek to live by maxims and those who want to go beyond the formulae. Her recurrent theme is the way in which being wrapped up in your own concerns blinds you to the co-ordinate existence of others. The conventions of her day forced her (like many nineteenth century novelists) to find ways of writing about sexuality by displacement. The rich results might make you speculate on the advantages of working under imposed difficulty.

Starting place: *The Mill on the Floss* (Penguin)

Further reading: *Middlemarch* (Penguin)

Fanthorpe, Ursula (b. 1929) A good entry point for those seeking to get in touch with contemporary poetry. UAF's poetry spans a variety of modes, and is notable for its humour, its modesty, and (generally) its accessibility. She manages to mix themes drawn from mythology with those drawn from everyday life and relationships, thus creating a re-framing effect. She also wrote some impressive poems about hospitals.

Selected Poems (Penguin)

Faulkner, William (1897–1962) One of many examples of a novelist putting the conflicts and guilts of American Southern History to imaginative use. In many ways an experimentalist, WF developed his own version of interior monologue, using multiple narrators to explore memory, the tropes by which people seek to hold fragmented experience together, the relations between siblings and generations, the working out of historical contradictions in the experience of families and individuals. His narrators tell and re-tell their stories, driven by obscure compulsions, and apparently doomed to keep repeating the past. Stylistically, this results in long sentences, and the scrambled chronology of those unable to let go of their own experience. All of this makes his novels difficult to read, but rewarding if you keep going.

> Starting place: *As I Lay Dying* (Penguin)
> Further reading: *The Sound and the Fury; Absalom, Absalom* (both Penguin)

Frost, Robert (1874–1963) While possibly the best known US poet of the century (at least on this side of the Atlantic), RF is included here for a poetry where the apparently stable persona, the speaking voice of the poet, whimsical, fairly easily understood, and full of wise sayings, is repeatedly dislodged by more sinister and less containable voices. RF's recurrent theme is an encounter, an occasion when a speaker or protagonist comes up against another person, or an event that throws their security into disarray – or at least breaks in upon their comfort.

> *Selected Poems* (Penguin)

Gaskell, Elizabeth (1810–65) Though we might sense with hindsight the limitations of EG's recipe for social harmony through mutual class understanding, we should not ignore her novels. Even 'great works' are not without undesirable ideological baggage. We need to 'read against the grain', and EG is a good example of the benefits of doing so. Her concern is the way in which class and education shape opportunity, and the shock experienced by those who step outside middle class comfort. Also deeply interested in the relations between generations. *Cranford* (perhaps too easily written off as slight) may be seen as an early study of a women's community.

> Starting place: *Wives and Daughters*
> Further reading: *North and South, Mary Barton, Cranford* (all in Penguin)

Glasgow, Ellen (1873–1945) The southern states of the USA seem to have produced novels rich in the complexity of the insertion of the individual drama into history. EG, too, is fascinated by the relations between subjective experience, and the historical patterns which such a life reproduces. Her themes are illusion, the power of repression in hiding away what you don't want to know about, and obsession with the past. In *The Sheltered Life* (which includes one of the most vigorous representations of ageing I know), she moves between viewpoints to create a brilliant and subtle drama of a society raised on illusion, foregrounding the cost of the dismissal of jarring or painful experience.

> Starting place: *The Sheltered Life*
> Further reading: *Barren Ground* (both Virago)

Goncharov, Ivan Aleksandrovich (1812–91) Here for the sake of *Oblomov* (Penguin), a rich and satisfying novel which can be read in a variety of ways. At a psychological level, it appears to be an acute study of depression, taking as its protagonist someone who rarely if he can help it gets out of bed, and whose friends infallibly get locked in 'helper' role. At another level it has been read allegorically as a study of the emotional/ moral defeat of the Russian governing classes in the mid-nineteenth century. But one might take such a reading more broadly as an account of the social aetiology of helplessness: the avoidance of change by denial.

Gordimer, Nadine (b. 1923) One thread running through these notes concerns the wealth of fiction produced in places where people are contending with the burdens of injustice and inequality. NG is a South African novelist whose novels struggle all the time with the relations between the personal and the political. Some novels (such as *Burger's Daughter*, and *A Sport of Nature*) explore the attempt to live a life devoted to bringing about change in the public domain. In others (e.g. *The Conservationist*) NG enters into an alien point of view to see how the subject as oppressor is shaped by its own history and generates its own utopias. Stylistically, her novels move between vivid realism, and interior dialogues, calling the reader into constructive effort. The plurality of voices creates problems for the reader/ interpreter who would like to find a secure viewpoint but cannot.

> Starting places: *Selected Stories; The Conservationist*
> Further reading: *Burger's Daughter, July's People* (all Penguin)

Hardy, Thomas (1840–1928) A prolific author of novels, poems, and short stories, TH merits inclusion for his struggles with a number of overlapping themes. These include the breakdown of traditional rural communities, the role of women, the experience of returning to your community as an outsider, and (above all in his poetry) the experience of loss and regret. Important insight into the injuries of class, and obsessional pursuit of ideals. TH explores the human implications of a universe not built around God's purposes, but one in which humans invest enormous emotion in places and objects. Time and again, he returns to the topos of being too late, of understanding attained when it is too late to do any good.

> Starting places: dip in poems (*Selected Poems*, Penguin), paying particular attention to 1913 poems. *Tess of the d'Urbervilles* (Penguin)
> Further reading: any of the later novels (e.g. *The Return of the Native, Jude the Obscure, The Woodlanders*); *Wessex Tales* (Penguin)

Harrison, Tony (b. 1937) In working with the conflicts arising from his education and his working class background, TH has proved himself a major poet of generational conflict and class mobility. His concern with the varieties of written and spoken language and the contradictions of culture leads him to poetic forms that can be grimly humorous at the same time as deeply pathetic. His poems on his father and mother and his own upbringing make a good starting place, since the reader can hold on to the preferred biographical thread. Formally, his poems exhibit a gaiety which then makes the content more of a shock.

> *Selected Poems* (Penguin)

Hartley, L.P. (1895–1972) Included here for his novel *The Go-Between* (Penguin), an intriguing study of growing up, and initiation into sexual knowledge. The framing of the novel foregrounds the transactions between memory and the past, inviting the reader into the construction of a life organised in a such a way as to avoid the pain which the past generated. Such a novel poses interesting questions about the relations between the narrator's and the reader's attempts to interpret what they see and hear.

Heaney, Seamus (b. 1939) Another poet whose work is forged out of the complexities of historical experience – here that of Northern Ireland. This is clearly such a recurrent theme of these notes that it is perhaps not necessary to assert that Heaney is a particularly good example of the reflective richness gained from locating individual emotion and experience within the archaeological layers of the past. The past thus resonates in two ways: as the familial past of the individual, and as the past of a culture. The dense sensory construction of SH's poems keeps the mind simultaneously active and resourced.

> Suggestions: dip in *Selected Poems* (Faber), and any of his collections. More recent volumes like *The Haw Lantern* and *Station Island* are more explicitly political.

Hoban, Russell (b. 1925) Though mainly known as a childrens' author, RH has also published several books for adults. Included here for *Riddley Walker* (Picador), which strikes me as a very serious account of adolescence. It is, however, much more than that, taking as its imaginary topography a post-holocaust England, where a society of survivors ekes out an existence, and tries to build a culture out of the fragments of the past that come their way. RH created a new dialect for his text, but the difficulties are well worth tackling.

Holtby, Winifred (1898–1935) A popular writer of the 1930s (and the subject of Vera Brittain's *Testament of Friendship*), who passed until recently into eclipse. Her novel *South Riding* (Virago) is a marvellous example of the persistence of the realist novel in locating persons and relationships within a political framework, so that her characters take part in a social drama without being devoid of a sense of inner life. Few twentieth century English novelists give such a formative account of the dynamics of community. Every story, WH proposes, interlocks with every other, so that as the reader passes back and forth he or she builds up an elaborate moving image of a society in action.

Holub, Miroslav (b. 1923) Included here to represent the wealth (if not the diversity) of Eastern European poetry, more of which is now available in translation than was the case a few years ago. What the English reader will find is a kind of poetry making that may seem at first rather alien, with its scientific imagery (MH is a research immunologist), its surrealism, its bizarre humour. If you hang on, you enter into a whole different way of coping with oppression, through coding, and through conceptual gymnastics. MH both seizes on sharp and bothering images, and tells elliptic little stories which come under the radar of the reader. His poems cannot easily be paraphrased or explained, and to that extent they are a challenge to a corresponding humour and agility in the response.

　　Poems Before and After (Bloodaxe)

Hughes, Ted (b.1926) A mainspring of his work seems to be the construction of a mythology, and many of his poems (and sequences) can be read as fragments towards such a mythology, attempting to bring together the natural and the human worlds, though in a way that defies sentimentalism. It is not a negative criticism to say that TH is obsessed with violence, though it seems to me that his violence (fragmenting, sadistic, eliminatory) could be seen as a very masculine form of expression. The poems in *Crow* seem to represent in their tortured language something of the disturbances of the dream.

　　Selected Poems 1957–1981 (Faber)

Ibsen, Henrik (1828–1906) Norwegian, but above all European playwright, pioneer of the new naturalistic theatre of the late nineteenth century. HI's plays generate their enormous power from the alternation between the poles of realism and symbolism, so that the action and the dialogue perpetually needs to be re-framed in the audience's mind. Passionate themes include the attempts of individuals to break out of claustrophobic circumstances, and the role of women in patriarchal middle class society. In IH's plays, domesticity is a trap (enacted in the furniture cluttered box-set), existing always in tension with a longed for energy and hope that is felt to exist somewhere in the untamed world outside.

HI is also of great interest because he raises for counsellors important questions about the effects unwittingly produced by those who attempt to open others' eyes and thereby destroy the 'life-lie' (the governing fiction) by which they have been living.

> Starting places: *Hedda Gabler; The Doll's House*
>
> Further reading: *The Master Builder; Rosmersholm; The Wild Duck* (all translated in both Methuen and Penguin). Or anything you can arrange to see.

James, Henry (1843–1916) I pondered over including reference to HJ's vast work here, and was swayed by his meticulous and enduring attention to exploitation in human relationships. He returns repeatedly to the ethical and psychological implications of the uses to which people put each other – which includes not alone manipulation by those we can identify as villains, but the way people get pushed into roles even by the kindly-disposed. HJ is also interested in the rationalisations and other stories people tell themselves about why their lives are as they are, and in the power parents and surrogate parents wield over young persons' lives (for example in *What Maisie Knew* and *The Turn of the Screw*). He is also fascinated by the figure of the questing, baffled interpreter, someone who tries often unsuccessfully to account for what they see around them, and in doing so anticipates the roles both of readers and counsellors.

> Starting places: (novels) *Washington Square, The Portrait of a Lady;* (stories) *The Jolly Corner and Other Stories;* (novella) *The Turn of the Screw*
>
> Further reading: *The Ambassadors* (all Penguin)

Joyce, James (1882–1941) JJ epitomises the twentieth century experience of exile (albeit often self-imposed), and the refractive light thus flung on your home and adoptive culture. A pioneer of the modernist revolt, JJ's work exemplifies the observation that finding new forms enlarges the zone of the sayable. From the point of view of the non-specialist reader, his work moves formally from the accessible (the stories in *Dubliners*) to the incomprehensible (*Finnegan's Wake*), where the attempt to outform form arguably leads to hermeticism – writing that is only comprehensible through a vast effort of exegesis. JJ's central enterprise is perhaps to invent a notation adequate to represent the subjective world of the individual, the feel and shape of that experience. The subjective world thus recorded demonstrates the self as collage, the internal drama of countless voices.

> Starting place: stories 'Eveline', 'A Painful Case', and 'The Dead' in *Dubliners; The Portrait of the Artist as a Young Man.*
>
> Further reading: *Ulysses* (all Penguin).

Kafka, Franz (1883–1924) A Czech novelist writing in the German of the Austrian rulers, FK's stories and novels construct a nightmarish world, which has led some critics to see him as a kind of twentieth century prophet. By distorting or overriding the conventions of realism, FK manages to probe deeply both into the fantasies through which power operates, and into the fear and paralysis of its victims. He explores our own complicity in evil. The world of his fiction is one where authority figures wield immense and capricious power, and where human solidarity seems unattainable. His work invites yet at the same time repels allegorical interpretation. Thus the novella *Metamorphosis* can be read as 'about' the way in which people treat handicap, though the story cannot be reduced to a single theme.

> Starting places: *Metamorphosis; The Trial*
>
> Further reading: dip in stories, for example 'In the Penal Colony' in *Collected Short Stories* (all Penguin).

Kelman, James (b.1946) Glaswegian novelist. In his novels and short stories JK has worked unceasingly at finding written languages to represent both working class speech and the dynamics of inner speech. His subjects are simultaneously victims of the society they inhabit and full of a defiant energy. He is particularly good at male relationships, and at the sort of relations with yourself that emerge from loneliness and isolation. And very funny.

> Starting place: any of the volumes of stories – e.g. *Not Not While the Giro* or *The Burn* (Minerva)
>
> Further reading: *The Busconductor Hines* (Phoenix); *A Disaffection* (Picador)

Larkin, Philip (1922–1985) The poet as social realist observer, PL creates a variety of characters and situations and peers into what lies behind them. His recurrent figures seem to be loneliness, exclusion, and stories of frustration. These are accessible poems which lead the reader into reflection upon the shaping of thought about desire, about what you feel is missing from your life, and about the fear of commitment to the ordinary. It would be a waste to reject them on the grounds of what is known of PL's own life.

> *Collected Poems* (Faber)

Lawrence, D.H. (1885–1930) Difficult working with the scale of DHL's output (poems, stories, novels, as well as criticism, essays, and travel books), and the scale of his reputation. Nowadays likely to be found exasperating on account of his intrusive narrative voice, hectoring tone, and deep ambivalence towards women. Yet these things should not prevent us from acknowledging his achievement in the field of human relations. His concern is with the sources of emotions, the play of complex, shifting, and often ambivalent forces to which we give convenient labels like love or hate. DHL seeks to track the inner workings of individuals' relationships to each other, and find ways of representing states and dynamics that defeat verbalisation as much as they defy tidy social arrangements. He is valuable to us for his unflagging efforts to get behind the words and behind the dialogue. It is striking that the attempt to speak for the penumbral shapes of desire leads in the direction of positing vast metaphysical forces. He is especially revealing on the relations between parents and children (e.g. *Sons and Lovers*), and he might interestingly be given a (consciously) male reading for his examination of the relations between his male characters. A lot of his most interesting work is to be found in his four dozen or so short stories.

Starting places: *Sons and Lovers*; dip in stories in *The Prussian Officer* and *England our England*
Further reading: *Selected poems*; other novels – *The Rainbow*; *Women in Love* (all Penguin)

Le Guin, Ursula (b. 1929) Science fiction is not all about hi-tech, nor am I even sure that Le Guin's adult work should be referred to as sci-fi. Creating imaginary worlds is only a few degrees further along the continuum from what all novelists do, and imaginary worlds provide models by which to judge human successes and failures in organising this one. The stance is that of the outsider looking in on the arrangements of other planets, but also sucked into involvement in those arrangements, with all their dubieties and dangers of gender, wealth, and power. The dispassionate (almost anthropological) observer cannot retain their detached role. Well worth looking at ULG's own essays in *Dancing at the Edge of the World* (Paladin).

Starting place: *The Left Hand of Darkness* (Futura)

Lessing, Doris (b. 1919) DL's prolific work moves between two poles: a form of intense realism with which she began and to which she has returned, and her enormous speculative/ futuristic novels of the 1970s. DL's first realistic phase led her to close quasi-autobiographical inwardness with her characters and thus further to decide that the only way to enquire into the wastage and damage that society generates was to look at the whole thing anew from the perspective of a new cosmos, organised by universal providers. *The Marriages between Zones Three, Four, and Five* seems to me the most accessible route into DL's futuristic world. It is also important to say that she is another product of southern Africa, and *The Grass is Singing* (set in what was then Rhodesia) is a good example of her work on humans in the autodestruct mode. Through it comes the question of where you turn for alternative possibilities. With enormous persistence she has worked away at this question, giving much attention to women and women's relationships as bearers of hope (e.g. the early *The Golden Notebook*). DL is a novelist of people on the edge, but with a strong sense that the edge may be the place from where positive change comes.

> Starting places: dip in the *Collected Short Stories*; for novels, try *The Grass is Singing*; *The Marriages between Zones Three, Four and Five* (Flamingo).

Levertov, Denise (b. 1923) British/American poet. DL commands a wide range of registers, from poems that are very visibly 'about' experiences, to poems that resonate with allusions. For me, DL raises the question of how far poets can manage without a domain approximating to the sacred, and how far (in the absence of such a publicly acknowledged domain) the poet finds it necessary to invent one, or at least sketch in what a world plunged in transcendent meaning would feel like. Is that part of the role of the secular poet? Can you write of human pain and the waste of potential without a horizon of hope? At all events, behind her everyday instances you may sense a reference to an order of experience that may have to be called by such a name as myth.

Selected Poems (Bloodaxe)

Levi, Primo (1919–1987) Having to draw lines somewhere, I haven't on the whole included principally non-fiction writers. PL's work seems to occupy such an important place in the hinterlands of fiction that I decided to include him, partly for the stunning autobiographical *If This is a Man* and *The Truce* about his experience of surviving Auschwitz, but also for his oblique fictions which invite the reader to conceptualise experience in new ways, and compose a useful antidote to blow-by-blow realism. *The Wrench* is that fairly rare thing, a novel which actually takes as its subject the world of work. (All Abacus)

Mann, Thomas (1875–1955) I struggled with the question of which European classics to include. In the end, the criterion had to be relevance to the goals of this book, and I am including Mann because of his enormous relevance to our narrative concerns. His novels locate his human subjects on a map of European culture and history, with a vivid enactment of the intersection between the individual's self-hypothesis and the larger social drama. Deeply committed to the liberal rationalist tradition, TM is absorbed by the effort to find out how reason and delusion consort, and destruction and evil enter into the culture. *The Magic Mountain* is, if not the best place to start, an enthralling study of institutionalisation.

> Starting places: *Death in Venice* (Penguin); explore short stories e.g. *Mario and the Magician and Other Stories* (Penguin)
> Going on to: *The Magic Mountain* (Penguin)

Mansfield, Katherine (1888–1923) Short story writer of marvellous economy and power. Wherever you enter her work, you will come across condensed narratives that summon the reader into filling out the world which surrounds them. Images recur of emergence from powerful relationships, of people (especially women) trying to cope with dignity with the loss of status, or making up roles for themselves out of pitiful fragments. This suggests (wrongly) that KM's stories are a lexicon of deficits: they are not, because of the energy called up in the very management of the material. She is of especial concern to to us because of her interest in point of view, and the mutual incomprehension arising between people of different class or status.

　　Collected Stories (Penguin)

Mason, Bobbie Ann (b. 1941) At one level BAM's stories are a transfixing account of lives lived on the margins of middle America. At another level, one might seem them as an account of dispossession, of people inhabiting a culture which seems to have lost any emblems of solidarity, or hope for the future, or even any sense of the past. Her short novel *In Country* takes as its subject the aftermath of the Vietnam War (although, one has immediately to add, the aftermath in the USA). One symptom of the moral desolation occupied by her characters is the apparent absence of awareness of what American policy might have wreaked elsewhere.

　　Starting place: stories in *Shiloh* (Flamingo)
　　Going on to: *In Country* (Flamingo); *Spence and Lila* (Vintage)

Morrison, Toni (b. 1931) Throughout these notes I have attempted to avoid being too specific about the cultural situations of authors and texts, in the hopes of sketching paradigms with force across the boundaries of cultures. But I can hardly fail to mention that TM's versions of growing up and of attempting to knit the individual and collective past derive from the experience of growing up black in the USA. In her novels, TM seems to have created a language to deal with the subjects of human endurance, humour, friendship, the capacity to bounce back against the weight of history. *Beloved* in particular is a deeply moving study of survival, solidarity, and story-telling.

　　Suggestions: *Sula* (Panther); *Beloved* (Picador); *Jazz* (Picador)

Muir, Edwin (1887–1959) The register of EM's poetry is allusive, evoking dream and myth. While he uses fairly recognisable forms, his poems approach the reader obliquely, inviting an attentive response as he or she seeks to fit together the powerful images which arise and which seem often to speak of inner conflict and states of the psyche, subjects of which it is inevitably hard to speak, and for which poetry can sometimes provide a language.

    Collected Poems (Faber)

    Further Reading: *An Autobiography* (Hogarth)

McCullers, Carson (1917–1967) Southern US novelist, one of so many produced by a region which has known defeat in war, CMcC's central theme is the reciprocal relations of solidarity and exclusion, the longings and terrors of those who want to belong. In *The Member of the Wedding* this is focused on an adolescent girl; other novels explore the tension between a haunting collection of outsiders and those who represent the community. Her texts are drawn between interior monologue and the weight of the outside narrator.

    Starting Place: *The Member of the Wedding*

    Further Reading: *The Heart is a Lonely Hunter; Clock without Hands* (Penguin)

O'Connor, Flannery (1925–1964) Southern US novelist and short story writer, FO'C constructs those moments at which peoples' own inner plots collide with their roles in others' dramas, moments often contrived through dynamic symbolism. Her stories can thus come to seem a rather unrelenting catalogue of exposures – characters stripped of their rationale and with it their dignity. But it seems to me that the tales which circulate around such moments – the moments when self-presentation falters – may have a particular bearing for those who attend to others as they try to adjust their own narratives. Her stories turn round the expectation of revelation. When that revelation comes it is different from what people expected.

    Starting Place: stories in *Everything That Rises Must Converge* (Faber)

Olsen, Tillie (b. 1913) TO has written sparingly, for reasons discussed in *Silences*, her own volume of essays and reflections. Here for her collection of (interlinked) stories *Tell me a Riddle* (Virago), stunning in their invention of forms adequate to their subject matter. In taking a family as her central thread, TO manages to suggest a work on a much larger scale than the brevity of the stories would lead you to expect. So thoroughly is the reader drawn in to the making, that acute emotional involvement is almost inevitable.

Piercy, Marge (b.1936) Here for *Woman on the Edge of Time* (Women's Press), another instance (cf. Lessing, Atwood) of the felt need to push beyond the boundaries of naturalism in the search for new shapes the self might assume, and new hopes for what culture and community could mean. Evidence perhaps that one drawback of fidelity to the actual is precisely its crushing force. If too close attention to the real saps hope, perhaps experiments like this of MP's are necessary if any sense of utopia is to be preserved and not simply diverted to consumerist ends by the forces of marketing. MP suggests powerfully (and even if you do not like her work) that humans *need* utopia to guide their humanness, and leaves with you the question of how in our time a visionary discourse can be achieved. How may we speak of hopes and possibilities except in the language of individual possession and achievement?

Pinter, Harold (b. 1930) 'Failure of communication' was the phrase that seemed to guide most conversations about HP's plays in the 1960s. If you see him as a kind of British Beckett, you realise that his apparently limited repertoire of instances of the failure to hear, delineates a bleak world where people seem deafened by the voices in their own heads, and incapable of attending to others. His territory is that composed of the banal objects with which people buttress their own security. He forces you to look at what sort of relatedness arises from subjects so apparently self-absorbed. We had better attend to HP's stage, which is a forum for thinking about what kind of sociality could happen in a social economy stripped of human solidarity and human listening.

Starting places: *The Homecoming; The Birthday Party; The Caretaker* (Methuen)

Plath, Sylvia (1932–63) It is difficult to see SP's work for her biography – or versions of it. This is a pity, since much of her poetry is very germane to our purposes. Her first person poems may be better read as dramatic roles than as statements from the 'I' of the poet. Like much of the poetry I have recommended, SP's arranges syntax and places images in such a way as to cause a rapid reading to snag, leading the reader back over it in an attempt to tease out sense. She seems to me a poet well worth bringing out from behind presuppositions about what she might be saying. SP offers a language for celebration and wonder as well as anger and fear, and a language for the investigation of the power of emotional drives.

Starting places: collections *Ariel* and *Crossing the Water* (Faber)
Further Reading: *Collected Poems* (Faber)

Rhys, Jean (1890–1979) Another example of the insight of the outsider – the writer/speaker approaching a culture from an oblique angle and the margins. JR's Caribbean provides a counter-example, a contrast to the London and Europe she so chillingly evokes. Her novels and stories evoke outsiders, wanderers, subjects displaced and trying to find their way in an unfamiliar culture. They also speak of finding your way as a woman, the ingenuity and surprising courage which those in need may discover. Homelessness is also a metaphor for the lack of support structure for those who try to go it alone.

Starting Place: *Good Morning Midnight*, stories in *Tigers are Better Looking*

Further reading: *Wide Sargasso Sea; After Leaving Mr Mackenzie* (all Penguin)

Smith, Ken (b. 1938) There are all sorts of good reasons for including KS as an example of some of the fine poetry of recent years. Particular reasons here have to do with his work on creating speaking voices for conditions of extreme loneliness, and as a sub-set, his poems on prisons and prisoners. His poems draw on and re-frame elements from popular culture, the news, episodes from daily life, suggesting as they do so the unconscious resonances of the episodes that jar on our daily attention. He is interested in fragments and bricolage, the experience on the other side of the easy story.

The Poet Reclining: Selected Poems 1962 – 1980; Wormwood (both Bloodaxe)

Smith, Stevie (1902–71) You should not be put off by SS's apparently fey and whimsical manner. Behind a jokey surface, and her use of jingley (though often disrupted) forms, she tackles a range of themes to do with woman–man relations, the difficulty of bridging your inner world and your public roles, the doubling back on themselves of emotions that lack expression. In addition to poetry, she wrote three novels. I recommend *Novel on Yellow Paper* (Virago) a semi-fictionalised autobiography which moves across a breath-taking range of registers. It is also very funny.

Stevie Smith, a Selection (Faber)

Stead, Christina (b. 1902) Included above all for the sake of her novel *The Man who Loved Children* (Penguin). This appears a huge rag-bag of a novel, but it may be that its feeling of being unedited actually arises because CS has delved further into the experience of family life than novelists have commonly been able to get at. The novel concerns the domination of his family by a hugely monomaniac (and right-on) father, and the attempts of his children, particularly his daughter, to break free. Vividly evokes adult relationships as experienced by children, and the drama of a man who moves dangerously between the desire to mould his children and his wish to be a marvellous child himself. So the novel also has a lot to tell us about masculinity.

Swift, Graham (b.1947) Best known for his novel *Waterland*, which is both a vivid evocation of growing up, and a case study in the search for adequate storytelling. The protagonist tries and tries again to get hold of the story of his own life, and then each part of the story in turn ramifies into others until he has conjured up a whole social environment. GS is preoccupied by relations between generations (particularly fathers and sons), and by how one generation seeks to influence and implant its own memory in another. He is thus concerned with the narrative mechanisms by which the past returns to haunt us. If you want to follow up *Waterland*, try the stories in *Learning to Swim*, or the novels *Shuttlecock*, or *The Sweet Shop Owner*. (All Picador.)

Tolstoy, Leo (1828–1910) While it is likely that any one who reads this book will probably have found their own way to LT, it is worth pointing out his relevance from the point of view of this book. From the vast expanse of his work, I would pick out stories like *The Death of Ivan Ilyich* and *The Kreutzer Sonata*. And if you haven't ever, do make time for *Anna Karenin*, which embeds themes of adultery, jealousy, the formation and rupturing of relationships within a working model of a whole society.

>   *The Death of Ivan Ilyich; The Kreutzer Sonata; Anna Karenin; War and Peace* (Penguin)

Walcott, Derek (b. 1930) DW's poetry works on a terrain where the experience of growing up black in the Caribbean, 'English', and classical cultures overlap. Draws on the different traditions available to him to weave an allusive and vivid poetry. Asks what it would mean to have a home base: the poet of movement between cultures as a condition of life.

>   *Poems 1948–1984* (Faber)

Walker, Alice (b. 1941) As will be evident from other entries, the experience of growing up black in the USA is clearly one that has produced some important novels. AW's work speaks not for black experience alone, but for all those who are attempting to build adequate lives in the face of exploitation, humiliation, and the sheer waste of human resources in a society divided by class or race. AW has found ways of telling of the potential brutality of the oppressed as well as their humour and vitality. She opens up the dilemma (inherent in the portrayal of oppressed groups) between naturalism and sentimentality.

>   Starting place: stories in *In Love and Trouble* (Women's Press)
>   Further Reading: *The Color Purple* (Women's Press)

Webb, Mary (1881–1927) Don't be put off by MW's 'provincial' reputation. Now above all we need access to worlds as yet untouched by metropolitan values and systems of communication. MW does not sentimentalise the society she represents, and her recurrent theme concerns women's attempts to break through its limits. Try either *Precious Bane* or *Gone to Earth* (both Virago).

Welty, Eudora (b. 1909) Southern US novelist and story writer. Included for her marvellous short stories, and for *The Optimist's Daughter*, a moving study of the relations between a daughter, her father, and the father's second wife. As you will have come to expect of southern novels, this also spells the family's connection with friends, and with a whole society against which it has built its barriers. Again and again, southern novels seem to put before us the theme of how an intimate unit like the family may try to protect itself from history, but how it is nevertheless in the end invaded by the very forces it sought to expel.

    The Optimist's Daughter (Virago); *Collected Stories* (Penguin)

White, Antonia (1898–1980) AW's chronicle of a girl growing into adulthood begins with an overbearing father and a convent school in *Frost in May*. The later volumes (*The Lost Traveller, The Sugar House*, and *Beyond the Glass* – all Virago) are harder going, but well worth the effort. AW's heroine is precariously perched on the edge of disintegration into madness. The painful detail is gathered around a form of telling which draws the reader into shocked collusion.

Woolf, Virginia (1882–1941) A novelist carrying out a quite self-consciously feminist programme (see *A Room of One's Own*) (Penguin), VW was committed to the attempt to achieve fidelity to the feel of life as you live it in the here and now. She was thus one of the pioneers of 'interior monologue', working out a form of narrative that would render the fluidity of perception and emotion, and represent the human subject not as a bundle of static and internally consistent qualities, but as the scene of inner conflict, inconsistency, the unpredictable advance and recoil of emotion. Whether or not she had hit upon a specifically feminine way of telling, VW models a way of thinking the inner life, but also a method for talking about the formative power of the patriarchal family.

    Starting Place: *To the Lighthouse*
    Further Reading: *The Waves; Between the Acts* (all Grafton)

Booklist

This is designed as a list of works which connect with the subject matter of this book. I hope it is of some use as a checklist of books which bear on the relation between counselling, psychotherapy and psychology, and the study of literature. The focus is on the uses of literature to therapy, and with a few exceptions I have not therefore attempted to represent the extensive domain of psychoanalytically-oriented literary criticism, or works of literary criticism in general. Some suggestions for further reading in the area of literary theory and criticism will be found at the end of the appropriate chapters.

Bakhtin, Mikhail (trans. Vern McGee) (1986) *Speech Genres and Other Late Essays*. Austin: University of Texas.
The essay 'The Problem of Speech Genres' crystallises much of the most relevant of MB's thinking. (See also Holquist and Todorov, below.)

Bettelheim, Bruno (1976) *The Uses of Enchantment: the Meaning and Importance of Fairy Tales*. London: Thames and Hudson.
A psychoanalytically informed account of fairy tales (and thus by implication other fictions) in the context of child development, and the treatment of disturbed children. Bettelheim considers the uses of fairy tales in relation to the resolution of unconscious conflict, and coming to terms with fantasies. His argument has been severely criticised by Maria Tatar in *Off With Their Heads! Fairy Tales and the Culture of Childhood* (Princeton N.J.: Princeton UP, 1992).

Bollas, Christopher (1987) *The Shadow of the Object: Psychoanalysis of the Unthought Known*. London: Free Association Books.
Builds on the object relations tradition to give an account of inner space that is very relevant here.

Bollas, Christopher (1989) *Forces of Destiny: Psychoanalysis and Human Idiom*. London: Free Association Books.
Connects with many of the issues discussed here.

Brooks, Peter (1994) *Psychoanalysis and Storytelling.* Oxford: Blackwell.
Brings together psychoanalysis and narrative theory in an illuminating way.
Sees transference as central to reading process.

Bruner, Jerome (1986) *Actual Minds, Possible Worlds.* Cambridge, Mass.:
Harvard University Press.
A great educationist explores the nature of learning in dialogue with others.

Burke, Kenneth (1937) 'Literature as Equipment for Living', reprinted in
(editors) Davis, Robert Con, and Finke, Laurie, *Literary Criticism and Theory.*
(1989) London: Longman.

Cox, Murray (Ed.) (1992) *Shakespeare Comes to Broadmoor: the Performance of
Tragedy in a Secure Psychiatric Hospital.* London: Jessica Kingsley Publishers.
Thought-provoking collection of materials generated by visits from members
of the RSC and RNT companies into Broadmoor and performances of major
productions there.

Cox, Murray, and Theilgaard, Alice (1987) *Mutative Metaphors in
Psychotherapy: the Aeolian Mode.* London: Tavistock.
Draws on literature, and a lot of thinking about metaphor and narrative, as
well as clinical experience to provide an absorbing account of work with
patients' discourse. MC and AT demonstrate powerfully one way in which the
therapist could draw on the experience of reading. Good bibliography.

Cox, Murray and Theilgaard, Alice (1994) *Shakespeare as Prompter: the
Amending Imagination and the Therapeutic Process.* London: Jessica Kingsley
Publishers.

Culler, Jonathan (1975) *Structuralist Poetics.* London: Routledge.
A pioneering work of synthesis which lucidly deciphers the relevance of
structuralist theories to the reading of all kinds of texts.

Easthope, Anthony (1989) *Poetry and Phantasy.* Cambridge: Cambridge
University Press.
A helpful guide, with detailed examples, to thinking about the relation
between poetry and the unconscious.

Ehrenzweig, Anton (1967) *The Hidden Order of Art.* London: Weidenfeld
and Nicolson (repr. in Paladin).
A brilliant psychoanalytic account of the creative process in connection with
twentieth century visual art. Especially interesting on the need to be able to
tolerate fragmentation and apparent failure.

Felman, Shoshana (1977) 'Turning the Screw of Interpretation' in *Yale French Studies 63.*
A ground-breaking essay on the transference involved in reading.

Gersie, Alida, and King, Nancy (1990) *Storymaking in Education and Therapy.* London: Jessica Kingsley Publishers.
A completely different emphasis from this book. Raises important questions about the relation between producing and living out stories.

GIlbert, Sandra M., and Gubar, Susan (1979) *The Madwoman in the Attic: The Woman Writer and the Nineteenth-Century Literary Imagination.* New Haven: Yale University Press.
One of the most influential works of literary criticism of recent years, G and G's great work invites us to re-think nineteenth century (and by implication more recent) literature in the light of their subtle analysis of the representation of women, and of the subterfuges available to the woman writer.

Gunn, Daniel (1988) *Psychoanalysis and Fiction: an Exploration of Literary and Psychoanalytic Borders.* Cambridge: Cambridge University Press.
Literary critical in orientation (readings of Kafka and Proust among others), this is useful as an example of a kind of Freudian approach that is following insight into the constitutive power of language and discourse.

Harding, Denys, W. (1963) *Experience into Words.* London: Chatto and Windus (repr. in Penguin).
A member of the first generation to be inspired by the possible application of Freudian insight to reading and literature, DWH wrote regrettably little. Many of his essays are collected here. All are worth reading, but I would recommend especially 'Reader and Author' and 'The Hinterland of Thought'.

Harré, Rom (2nd. edn. 1993) *Social Being.* Oxford: Blackwell.
An account of social life in terms of discursive events by one of the pioneers of the social constructionist school.

Henriques, Julian and Others (1984) *Changing the Subject: Psychology, Social Regulation and Subjectivity.* London: Methuen.
Provocative set of essays on the discourses (educational and psychological) among which the self is shaped.

Hillman, James (1983) *Healing Fiction.* Barrytown, N.Y.: Station Hill Press.
Oriented to analytical practice. Consists of discussions of Freud, Jung, and Adler in terms of the narrative strengths of each school. Re-telling your own story is itself therapeutic, and can be enriched by knowledge of myths and written fictions.

Hobson, Robert (1985) *Forms of Feeling; the Heart of Psychotherapy*. London: Tavistock.
A detailed account of psychotherapeutic practice informed by a wide interest in metaphor and poetry.

Holland, Norman (1975) *The Dynamics of Literary Response*. New York: W.W. Norton.
An extended piece of psychoanalytic literary criticism, working above all with the way in which fantasy can be managed in the literary text. Unlike earlier Freudian critics, Holland is not interested so much in the author as case-history as in the work performed by the reader.

Holquist, Michael (1990) *Dialogism: Bakhtin and His World*. London: Methuen.
An exposition of Mikhail Bakhtin's thought which raises central questions about social, educational, and therapeutic relations.

Humphrey, Nicholas (1986) *The Inner Eye*. London: Faber/Channel 4.
A popular account of the nature and uses of human consciousness, and the various reflexive means (including literature) that we use to 'do psychology' in the everyday.

Kermode, Frank (1967) *The Sense of an Ending: Studies in the Theory of Fiction*. London: Oxford University Press.
A wide-ranging exploration of the story-telling compulsion in the light of the need to establish security by shaping endings. Narrative endows events with meaning by forming them into coherent patterns.

Knights, Ben (1992) *From Reader to Reader: Theory, Text and Practice in the Study Group*. Hemel Hempstead: Harvester Wheatsheaf.
Primarily addressed to teachers of English and related subjects, this book tries to construct a theory about reading which draws on the group relations tradition.

Knights, L.C. (1980) 'Poetry and 'Things Hard for Thought'', *International Review of Psychoanalysis 7*, reprinted in *Selected Essays in Criticism*. Cambridge: Cambridge University Press.

Lakoff, George, and Johnson, Mark (1980) *Metaphors We Live By*. Chicago: University of Chicago Press.
Already much-referred to in these pages, this is a valuable (if sometimes over-schematic) investigation of the role of metaphor in the daily construction of reality.

Lakoff, George, and Turner, Mark (1989) *More Than Cool Reason: a Field Guide to Poetic Metaphor.* Chicago: Chicago University Press.
A development of GL and MJ's earlier book to explore the structures of poetic metaphor, and the creative ways in which metaphors can be stretched and re-made. Helpfully analyses a number of poetic examples.

Leedy, Jack. J. (editor) (1969) *Poetry Therapy: the Use of Poetry in the Treatment of Emotional Disorders.* Philadelphia: Lippincott.
A very mixed batch of essays on a subject related to the field of this book — the uses of writing and reading with the emotionally disturbed. Perhaps as a result of its institutional origins the book generally seems to take a clean-cut, no-nonsense approach to matters of 'mental hygiene'.

McGregor, Graham, and White, R.S. (editors) (1986) *The Art of Listening.* London: Croom Helm.
Essays which in crossing the boundary between therapy and literary study complement in many ways the subject matter of this book.

Mair, Miller (1989) *Between Psychology and Psychotherapy: a Poetics of Experience.* London: Routledge.
A clinical psychologist and psychotherapist, MM seeks to invent a discourse more adequate to talk about the experience of healing than that of positivistic science. In doing so (and risking the vulnerability which results from a more personal and exploratory form of writing), he draws on the resources of poetry and metaphor to start to think through the inter-personal processes of therapy.

Milner, Marion (also published as Joanna Field) (1950) *On Not Being Able to Paint.* (reprinted) London: Heinemann.
A fascinating and also deeply personal inquiry into the mutual relations between art and therapy.

Milner, Marion (1987) *Eternity's Sunrise: a Way of Keeping a Diary.* London: Virago.
A richly fertile exploration of the function of symbolism in the individual life by the author of *A Life of One's Own* and *An Experiment in Leisure.*

Potter, Jonathan, Stringer, Peter and Wetherell, Margaret (1984) *Social Texts and Context.* London: Routledge.
Interested in the reciprocal light that literature and social psychology can throw on each other. Studies the discursive forms through which sense-making takes place.

Read, Herbert (1960) *The Forms of Things Unknown: Essays Towards an Aesthetic Philosophy*. London: Faber.
HR was one of the seminal thinkers on the relations between art and psycho-analysis of the years immediately before and after the second world war. These essays, which draw on Jung as much as Freud, provide an account of art in terms of the exploration and fulfilment of profound human needs.

Rimmon-Kenan, Shlomith (editor) (1987) *Discourse in Psychoanalysis and Literature*. London: Methuen.
A variable collection of essays, some of which pursue a good deal further questions which are raised here.

Rose, Jacqueline (1984) *The Case of Peter Pan: or the Impossibility of Children's Fiction*. London: Macmillan.
A critical examination of the way in which the child and childhood is constructed in fiction written for children. Relevant here as an example of the analysis of the ideological work performed by texts.

Rosenblatt, Louise (1978) *The Reader, the Text, the Poem: the Transactional Theory of the Literary Work*. Carbondale: Southern Illinois University Press.
An indefatigable exponent of the creative adventure of readers, LR puts forward a compelling thesis about the web readers weave between themselves and the text. In her insistence that the text is also a medium of communication between readers she comes very close to our concerns here.

Rowan, John (1990) *Subpersonalities; the People Inside Us*. London: Routledge.
I have a lot of worries about JR's argument, but am in no doubt that a theory of subpersonalities is both useful, and pertinent to any attempt to think about the relations between the self and what we read. A useful introduction.

Rowe, Dorothy (1987) *Beyond Fear*. London: Fortana/Collins.

Sedgwick, Eve Kosofsky (1985) *Between Men: English Literature and Male Homosocial Desire*. New York: Columbia UP.
Another work whose scope goes far beyond literary criticism to explore the patterns of bonding and exclusion celebrated and reinforced – but also called into question – through cultural texts.

Sellers, Susan (editor) (1989) *Delighting the Heart: a Notebook by Women Writers*. London: The Women's Press.
An anthology of reflections on writing which raises any number of issues about creativity and the social channels available to the imagination.

Shotter, John, and Gergen, Kenneth J. (editors) (1989) *Texts of Identity.* London: Sage.
A handy collection of readings on the construction of the self through discourse – variations on the insight that we 'are' the stories we tell about ourselves.

Shotter, John (1993) *Cultural Politics of Everyday Life: Social Constructionism, Rhetoric and Knowing of the Third Kind.* Buckingham: Open University Press.
In many ways a difficult book, embedding a mass of quotation. But as a deeply suggestive account of life as lived in perpetual dialogue it has a lot to say to our concerns.

Showalter, Elaine (1985) *The Female Malady: Women, Madness and English Culture 1830–1980.* London: Virago.
An absorbing and at times horrifying investigation into how cultural images – here of femininity and suitable womanly behaviour – have shaped perception and practice.

Siegelbaum, Ellen, Y. (1990) *Metaphor and Meaning in Psychotherapy.* New York: Guilford Press.
Seeks to rescue primary process from the rationalism that sees it as merely regressive or pathological. Locates therapy in the common ground shared by therapist and client.

Sontag, Susan (1979) *Illness as Metaphor.* London: Allen Lane.
For anyone interested in the therapeutic uses of language and metaphor this is a challenging and suggestive book.

Smail, David (1984) *Illusion and Reality: the Meaning of Anxiety.* London: Dent.
I find myself constantly going back to DS who is deeply interested in language and communication, but also in the material contexts in which they take place.

Tanner, Tony (1979) *Adultery and the Novel: Contract and Transgression.* Baltimore, MD: Johns Hopkins.
An excellent example of an approach to the reading of literature that studies how fiction explores social contradictions and dilemmas. TT takes adultery as a metaphor, and follows through the issues that the metaphor focuses.

Todorov, Tzvetan (translated by Wald Godzich) (1984) *Mikhail Bakhtin: the Dialogical Principle.* Manchester: Manchester University Press.
Summarises those aspects of the work of MB (the collaborative and dialogic nature of narrative) that are most relevant for present purposes.

Warner, Marina (1994) *Managing Monsters: Six Myths of Our Time*. London: Vintage.
MW's Reith Lectures bring formidable cultural and historical knowledge to bear on contemporary thought. Connects with arguments of this book through her concern with finding stories that might transform rather than simply reproduce beliefs. The 'process of understanding and clarification... can give rise to newly told stories, can sew and weave and knit different patterns into the social fabric...'

Watzlawick, Paul (1978) *The Language of Change: Elements of Therapeutic Communication*. New York: Basic Books.
Brings together traditions originating with Gregory Bateson and with Transactional Analysis. Approach therefore very different from that implied here.

White, M. and Epston, D. (1990) *Narrative Means to Therapeutic Ends*. New York: W.W. Norton

Williams, Meg Harris, and Waddell, Margot (1991) *The Chamber of Maiden Thought: Literary Origins of the Psychoanalytic Model of the Mind*. London: Routledge.
Sets going many ideas about poetry and the unconscious, although I am not sure the book does what it sets out to do.

Winnicott, D.W. (1971) *Playing and Reality*. London: Tavistock.
Reflections on the role of creative play in the search for the self by one of Britain's greatest psychoanalytic thinkers. DWW sketches also the implications for the making and reading of cultural works of his theory of the 'potential space'.

Wright, Elizabeth (1984) *Psychoanalytic Criticism: Theory in Practice*. London: Routledge.
A useful short guide to the ways in which psychoanalytic thinking has been adopted into literary studies.

Young, Katherine Galloway (1987) *Taleworlds and Storyrealms: the Phenomenology of Narrative*. Dordrecht: Martinus Nijhoff.
Uses narratological methods to analyse oral storytelling. The notion of the 'taleworld' (the context in which the story is told), and the 'storyrealm' (the matter of the story) is highly pertinent to our subject. 'Relationships between events in the Taleworld can be reinvestigated as relationships between elements in the Storyrealm' p.214).

The Train from Rhodesia

The train came out of the red horizon and bore down towards them over the single straight track.

The stationmaster came out of his little brick station with its pointed chalet roof, feeling the creases in his serge uniform in his legs as well. A stir of preparedness rippled through the squatting native venders waiting in the dust; the face of a carved wooden animal, eternally surprised, stuck out of a sack. The stationmaster's barefoot children wandered over. From the grey mud huts with the untidy heads that stood within a decorated mud wall, chickens, and dogs with their skin stretched like parchment over their bones, followed the piccanins down to the track. The flushed and perspiring west cast a reflection, faint, without heat, upon the station, upon the tin shed marked 'Goods', upon the walled kraal, upon the grey tin house of the stationmaster and upon the sand, that lapped all around from sky to sky, cast little rhythmical cups of shadow, so that the sand became the sea, and closed over the children's black feet softly and without imprint.

The stationmaster's wife sat behind the mesh of her veranda. Above her head the hunk of a sheep's carcass moved slightly, dangling in a current of air.

They waited.

The train called out, along the sky; but there was no answer; and the cry hung on: I'm coming... I'm coming...

The engine flared out now, big, whisking a dwindling body behind it; the track flared out to let it in.

Creaking, jerking, jostling, gasping, the train filled the station.

Here, let me see that one – the young woman curved her body farther out of the corridor window. Missus? smiled the old man, looking at the creatures he held in his hand. From a piece of string on his grey finger hung a tiny woven basket; he lifted it, questioning. No, no, she urged, leaning down towards him, across the height of the train towards the man in the piece of old rug; that one, that one, her hand commanded. It was a lion, carved out of soft dry wood that looked like spongecake; heraldic, black and white, with impressionistic detail burnt in. The old man held it up to her still smiling, not from the heart, but at the customer. Between its vandyke teeth, in the mouth opened in an endless roar too terrible to be heard, it had a black tongue. Look, said the young husband, if you don't mind! And round the neck of the thing, a piece of fur (rat? rabbit? meerkat?); a real mane, majestic, telling you somehow that the artist had delight in the lion.

All up and down the length of the train in the dust the artists sprang, walking bent, like performing animals, the better to exhibit the fantasy held towards the faces on the train. Buck, startled and stiff, staring with round black and white eyes. More lions, standing erect, grappling with strange, thin, elongated warriors who clutched spears and showed no fear in their slits of eyes. How much, they asked from the train, how much?

Give me penny, said the little ones with nothing to sell. The dogs went and sat, quite still, under the dining car, where the train breathed out the smell of meat cooking with onion.

A man passed beneath the arch of reaching arms meeting grey-black and white in the exchange of money for the staring wooden eyes, the stiff wooden legs sticking up in the air; went along under the voices and the bargaining, interrogating the wheels,. Past the dogs; glancing up at the dining car where he could stare at the faces, behind glass, drinking beer, two by two, on either side of a uniform railway vase with its pale dead flower. Right to the end, to the guard's van, where the stationmaster's children had just collected their mother's two loaves of bread; to the engine itself, where the stationmaster and the driver stood talking against the steaming complaint of the resting beast.

The man called out to them, something loud and joking. They turned to laugh, in a twirl of steam. The two children careered over the sand, clutching the bread, and burst through the iron gate and up the path through the garden in which nothing grew.

Passengers drew themselves in at the corridor windows and turned into compartments to fetch money, to call someone to look. Those sitting inside looked up: suddenly different, caged faces, boxed in, cut off after the contact of outside. There was an orange a piccanin would like... What about that chocolate? It wasn't very nice...

A girl had collected a handful of the hard kind, that no one liked, out of the chocolate box, and was throwing them to the dogs, over at the dining car. But the hens darted in and swallowed the chocolates, incredibly quick and accurate, before they had even dropped in the dust, and the dogs, a little bewildered, looked up with their brown eyes, not expecting anything.

— No, leave it, said the young woman, don't take it...

Too expensive, too much, she shook her head and raised her voice to the old man, giving up the lion. He held it high where she had handed it to him. No, she said, shaking her head. Three-and-six? insisted her husband, loudly. Yes baas! laughed the old man. *Three-and-six?* – the young man was incredulous. Oh leave it – she said. The young man stopped. Don't you want it? he said, keeping his face closed to the old man. No, never mind, she said, leave it. The old native kept his head on one side, looking at them sideways, holding the lion. Three-and-six, he murmured, as old people repeat things to themselves.

The young woman drew her head in. She went into the coupé and sat down. Out of the window, on the other side, there was nothing; sand and bush; a thorn tree. Back through the open doorway, past the figure of her husband in the corridor, there was the station, the voices, wooden animals waving, running feet. Her eye followed the funny little valance of scrolled wood that outlined the chalet roof of the station; she thought of the lion and smiled. That bit of fur round the neck. But the wooden buck, the hippos, the elephants, the baskets that already bulked out of their brown paper under the seat and on the luggage rack! How will they look at home? Where will you put them? What will they mean away from the places you found them? Away from the unreality of the last few weeks? The young man outside. But he is not part of the unreality; he is for good now. Odd... somewhere there was an idea that he, that living with him, was part of the holiday, the strange places.

Outside, a bell rang. The stationmaster was leaning against the end of the train, green flag rolled in readiness. A few men who had got down to stretch their legs sprang onto the train, clinging to the observation platforms, or perhaps merely standing on the iron step, holding the rail; but on the train, safe from the one dusty platform, the one tin house, the empty sand.

There was a grunt. The train jerked. Through the glass the beer drinkers looked out, as if they could not see beyond it. Behind the fly-screen, the stationmaster's wife sat facing back at them beneath the darkening hunk of meat.

There was a shout. The flag drooped out. Joints not yet coordinated, the segmented body of the train heaved and bumped back against itself. It began to move; slowly the scrolled chalet moved past it, the yells of the natives, running alongside, jetted up into the air, fell back at different levels. Staring wooden faces waved drunkenly, there, then gone, questioning for the last time at the windows. Here, one-and-six baas! — As one automatically opens a hand to catch a thrown ball, a man fumbled wildly down his pocket, brought up the shilling and sixpence and threw them out; the old native, gasping, his skinny toes splaying the sand, flung the lion.

The piccanins were waving, the dogs stood, tails uncertain, watching the train go: past the mud huts, where a woman turned to look up from the smoke of the fire, her hand pausing on her hip.

The stationmaster went slowly in under the chalet.

The old native stood, breath blowing out the skin between his ribs, feet tense, balanced in the sand, smiling and shaking his head. In his opened palm, held in the attitude of receiving, was the retrieved shilling and sixpence.

The blind end of the train was being pulled helplessly out of the station.

The young man swung in from the corridor, breathless. He was shaking his head with laughter and triumph. Here! he said. And waggled the lion at her. One-and-six!

What? she said.

He laughed. I was arguing with him for fun, bargaining — when the train had pulled out already, he came tearing after... One-and-six Baas! So there's your lion.

She was holding it away from her, the head with the open jaws, the pointed teeth, the black tongue, the wonderful ruff of fur facing her. She was looking at it with an expression of not seeing, of seeing something different. Her face was drawn up, wryly, like the face of a discomforted child. Her mouth lifted nervously at the corner. Very slowly, cautious, she lifted her finger and touched the mane, where it was joined to the wood.

But how could you, she said. He was shocked by the dismay of her face.

Good Lord, he said, what's the matter?

If you wanted the thing, she said, her voice rising and breaking with the shrill impotence of anger, why didn't you buy it in the first place? If you wanted it, why didn't you pay for it? Why didn't you take it decently, when he offered it? Why did you have to wait for him to run after the train with it, and give him one-and-six? One-and-six!

She was pushing it at him, trying to force him to take the lion. He stood astonished, his hands hanging at his sides.

But you wanted it! You liked it so much?

– It's a beautiful piece of work, she said fiercely, as if to protect it from him.

You liked it so much! You said yourself it was too expensive –

Oh *you* – she said, hopeless and furious. *You* ... She threw the lion on to the seat.

He stood looking at her.

She sat down again in the corner and, her face slumped in her hands, stared out of the window. Everything was turning round inside her. One-and-six. One-and-six. One-and-six for the wood and the carving and the sinews of the legs and the switch of the tail. The mouth open like that and the teeth. The black tongue, rolling, like a wave. The mane round the neck. To give one-and-six for that. The heat of shame mounted through her legs and body and sounded in her ears like the sound of sand pouring. Pouring, pouring. She sat there, sick. A weariness, a tastelessness, the discovery of a void made her hands slacken their grip, atrophy emptily, as if the hour was not worth their grasp. She was feeling like this again. She had thought it was something to do with singleness, with being alone and belonging too much to oneself.

She sat there not wanting to move or speak, or to look at anything, even; so that the mood should be associated with nothing, no object, word or sight that might recur and so recall the feeling again... Smuts blew in grittily, settled on her hands. Her back remained at exactly the same angle, turned against the young man sitting with his hands drooping between his sprawled legs, and the lion, fallen on its side in the corner.

The train had cast the station like a skin. It called out to the sky, I'm coming, I'm coming; and again, there was no answer.

(Nadine Gordimer 1953)

References

Behr, H.L. (1988) A group analytic contribution to family therapy. *Journal of Family Therapy*, vol 10.

Blake, W. (1793) *Songs of Innocence and Experience*. In J. Keynes (ed) (1969) *Blake: Complete Writings*. London: Oxford University Press.

Booth, S. (1969) *An Essay on Shakespeare's Sonnets*. New Haven, CT: Yale University Press.

Bruner, J. (1982) *On Knowing: Essays for the Left Hand*. Third edition. Cambridge, MA: Harvard University Press.

Eliot, G. (1858) *Scenes of Clerical Life*. Harmondsworth: Penguin (1973).

Flaubert, G. (1854) *Madame Bovary*. Harmondsworth: Penguin (1951).

Fontane, T. (1894) *Effi Briest*. (Translated by Douglas Parmée.) Harmondsworth: Penguin (1967).

Greene, G. (1938) *Brighton Rock*.

Hines, B. (1968) *Kes (A Kestrel for a Knav)*. Harmondsworth: Penguin.

Sillitoe, A. (1959) *The Loneliness of the Long Distance Runner*. London: Grafton

Webster, R. (1990) *A Brief History of Blasphemy*. Southwold: The Orwell Press.

Subject
Index

referential model of
    language 20–1
re-framing 18, 30, 49
    metaphor 62–3
    narrative 68, 70, 89
'register' 23
Reisz, Mlle, *The Awakening*
    102–3
relationships, *The*
    Awakening 101–4
repetition 33, 56–7, 82
repression 6, 80
'reproduction' 3
re-telling of stories 89
rhyme 42–4
roles, *The Awakening*
    101–4
rules, in narratives 76
Runaway Soul 12

Scenes of Clerical Life 86
sea symbols, *The*
    Awakening 104–5
selection, in narrative 71
self-responsibility goals,
    and re-framing 18
semes 96
semiology/semiotics *see*
    signs
sentences
    narrative analogy 75
    transitivity 19
serious nature of literature
    114
'serious play' 42–3, 44
'shadow awareness of
    inferiority' 2
shaping *see* form in
    narrative
short chapters 97
Shorter Oxford English
    Dictionary 59
'sibling relations' themes
    125
signification 12–13,
    23–4, 38, 39, 105

'signified' 13
'signifiers' 13, 104–9
signs 12–13, 23–4
    arbitrary nature of 14
slow reading 27, 40
social contexts 21, 22
    of narratives 73, 80
    The Awakening 107–8
    Train from Rhodesia 34–5
social fantasies 38, 80
social performance,
    language as 12, 13, 21
'social self as garment'
    metaphor 108–9
Songs of Experience 31–2
Sonnet 73 51–2, 64
Sons and Lovers 93
'Soul has Bandaged
    Moments, The' 66
Sound and the Fury, The 91
sound patterns, in poetry
    41, 42–3, 45, 56–7
speaker-listener
    relationships 11–12
'speech act theory' 20
starting off, *The Awakening*
    96–7
stereotypes 102
stories *see* narrative
'stream of consciousness'
    91
structure *see* form
style, linguistic 16–20
'subject-centred causation'
    formulae 73–4
subjective/objective status
    of fiction 39
'Surprised by joy' 46
suspense, in narrative 76
symbolic deprivation 4
symbolism 24–5, 33, 36,
    38, 63–4, 81, 84
    The Awakening 104–9
syntax 16–17, 19
sympathy theory 90–1

systemic nature of
    metaphor 60

'technologies of discourse'
    3
'terministic screens' 59
texts *see* literary texts
themes 82, 106
    list 113–26
therapeutic culture 1, 3,
    70–1
thinking 5
    analogical 6, 49–53
    language and 14–15,
        17–19
    poem formation 45
third person narration
    86–7, 91, 96
time processes, in
    narrative 69, 73
'To Speak of Sorrow'
    45–6
To the Lighthouse 91–2, 93
topics 7, 113–26
topographical model of
    mind 39
topos of disclosure, *The*
    Awakening 98, 104
'traditional community
    break up' themes
    125–6
traditional narrators,
    counsellors compared
    91
Train from Rhodesia 33–6,
    37–8, 156–9
'transactional self' 2
transformational grammar
    18
transitivity 19–20
tropes 74–5
truth/fiction distinction
    69, 80
'type', 'figure' compared
    101, 102

Author Index